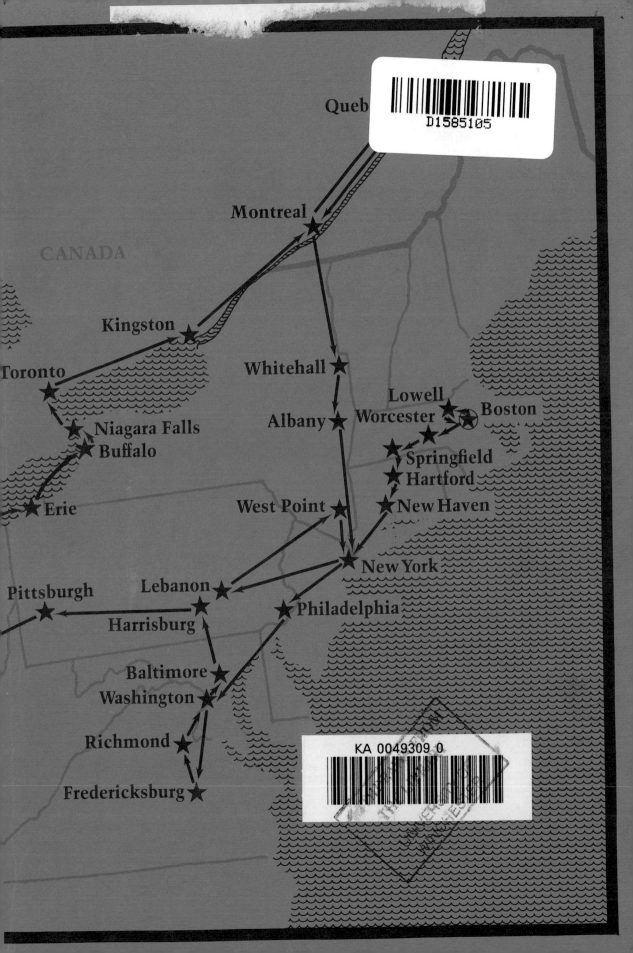

Queb

Montreal

CANADA

Kingston

Toronto

Whitehall

Niagara Falls

Buffalo

Lowell

Albany   Worcester   Boston

Springfield

Hartford

Erie

West Point   New Haven

Pittsburgh   Lebanon   New York

Harrisburg   Philadelphia

Baltimore

Washington

Richmond

Fredericksburg

Dickens on America and the Americans

Dickens

on America & the Americans

Edited by Michael Slater

 The Harvester Press

ISBN 0-85527-744-0

Copyright © 1979 by The Harvester Press Ltd.

Printed in United States of America

Picture research: James Dee Logan
Illustration credits:
T. W. Tyrell Collection at the Dickens House
  Museum, London, by permission of the Trustees
  at Dickens House: pages 5, 6, 7, 10, 11, 13, 14,
  16–17, 18, 24, 25, 28, 29, 50–51, 53, 54, 56, 57, 59,
  60, 62, 63, 65, 66, 73, 74, 83, 84, 88, 138, 154, 174,
  218, 223, 224, 231, 236, 237, 244
Humanities Research Center, the University of
  Texas at Austin: pages 15, 55, 58, 72, 77, 90, 95,
  106–107, 111, 116–117, 120–121, 144–145, 164,
  206, 222, 226, 240–241, 246
I. N. Phelps Stokes Collection of American
  Historical Prints, the New York Public Library:
  pages 141, 162–163
Eno Collection, the New York Public Library:
  pages 180–181

CONTENTS

Acknowledgments and editorial note ix

Introduction 1

I. First impressions: letters from America, 1842

1. Meeting the press 71
2. Utopia – apparently 72
3. National vanity 73
4. Home truths 75
5. Complaints of a Lion 76
6. American ladies. Liberty endangered 78
7. American railroads 79
8. A visit to the president 81
9. Congressmen 84
10. The American character 85
11. Slavery 86
12. Further complaints of a Lion 88
13. "Not the Republic of my imagination" 89
14. A smart youngster 91
15. Life on a canal boat 92
16. A depressing landscape 94
17. "Fixing" the Queen's English 96
18. A diseased body politic 97
19. Bores 97
20. A Cincinnati temperance festival 99
21. On the Mississippi 102
22. Slavery and its defenders 103
23. The prairie 105
24. St. Louis society 107
25. A corduroy road 108
26. Midwestern manners 109
27. International copyright again 110

II. *American Notes*

CITIES

28. Boston 115
29. New York: Wall Street 119
30. New York: the Five Points 119
31. Philadelphia 125
32. Washington 127
33. Richmond 129
34. Pittsburgh 131
35. Cincinnati 131

LANDSCAPES

36. New England 137
37. Virginia: Fredericksburg
to Richmond 139
38. The banks of the
Mississippi 140
39. Niagara 142

INSTITUTIONS

40. Law courts 146
41. A lunatic asylum 148
42. The press 149

SOCIAL LIFE AND MANNERS

43. Amusements of the ladies
of Boston 151
44. Communal meals on a canal
boat 154
45. A roadside conversation
155

CHARACTERS

46. Factory girls 158
47. Broadway loungers
(porcine) 160
48. Congressmen 161
49. A Mississippi man 166
50. An Indian chief 167
51. A midwestern couple 170
52. The Shakers 170
53. The "artist in boots" 173

NATIONAL CHARACTERISTICS

54. "An innumerable brood of evils" 176

III. *Martin Chuzzlewit*

55. The New York press 180
56. A patriot 183
57. At table – and afterward 183
58. A cultivated family 185
59. A social catastrophe 186
60. Feminine pastimes 189
61. Martin instructed regarding
his Queen's habitation 190
62. The Watertoast
Sympathisers 192
63. Martin lionised 194
64. National self-justification
197
65. The settlement of Eden 198
66. A child of Freedom 199
67. The Pogram Defiance 201
68. Literary ladies 203
69. The travellers' valediction
205

IV. Letters and writings, 1844 to 1855

70. The American press 209
71. American justice 210
72. An American panorama 211
73. An American in Europe 214
74. A new issue of *American Notes* 215
75. "That other Public" in America 216
76. Remembering American inns 218

V. Second impressions: letters and farewell speech, 1867/68

77. Boston revisited 222
78. Dining customs 223
79. New York revisited 225
80. Railroads, policemen, and newspapers 227
81. Contrasts 228
82. Changes 229
83. Baltimore postbellum 232
84. The Ghost of Slavery 235
85. President Johnson 237
86. Syracuse 238
87. Buffalo 239
88. Last words in America 242

Acknowledgments and editorial note

The texts of all but five of the extracts from Dickens' letters in section I of this anthology are taken from John Forster's *Life of Dickens* (ed. J. W. T. Ley, London: Cecil Palmer, 1928); extracts 8, 12, 13, and 18 are taken from *The Pilgrim Edition of the Letters of Charles Dickens*, vol. 3 (ed. Madeline House, Graham Storey, and Kathleen Tillotson, Oxford: Clarendon Press, 1978), and are reprinted here by permission of Oxford University Press. The Forster letters all appear, more accurately edited, in the *Pilgrim Edition*.

In the second section, I have grouped the extracts from *American Notes* by subject. They appear here, therefore, in an order different from that in which they appear in the actual volume.

Extracts 70 and 71 in section IV are taken from *The Pilgrim Edition of the Letters of Charles Dickens*, vol. 4 (ed. Kathleen Tillotson, Oxford: Clarendon Press, 1978), and are reprinted here by permission of Oxford University Press. Extract 88 in section V is taken from *The Speeches of Charles Dickens* (ed. K. J. Fielding, Oxford: Clarendon Press, 1960) and is reprinted here by permission of Oxford University Press. The extracts from Dickens' letters in section V are taken from *The Letters of Charles Dickens* (ed. W. Dexter, Bloomsbury: Nonesuch Press, 1938).

I wish to record my gratitude to the following friends for much help and advice during the compilation of this work: Professor Ashby Bland Crowder of Hendrix College, Arkansas, Mary Ford, and Douglas Johnson. I am grateful, too, to Barbara Brunswick for her excellent typing work and to Holly Carver of the University of Texas Press for a superb job of copy editing.

M.S.

INTRODUCTION

Michael Slater

I

America was the China of the nineteenth century – described, analyzed, promoted, and attacked in virtually every nation struggling to come to terms with new social and political forces. Sure of her destiny, she commanded international attention. The Declaration of Independence appealed to the conscience of the world, the Revolution enlisted international support, and the Constitution thrust an unknown political personality into the society of nations. What had been a somewhat obscure, occasionally romanticized backwater of colonial exploitation became, virtually overnight, a phenomenon to be investigated, a political and moral experiment to be judged. Throughout the following century thousands of foreign visitors – reporters, social critics, and artists among them – took up the challenge.[1]

The big difference between nineteenth-century America and present-day China, from the point of view of Mr. Pachter's illuminating comparison, lies in the word "thousands." America was wide open to curious foreigners, whether they came simply to observe or with some ulterior motive. Among the British visitors many, like the retired sailors Captains Basil Hall and Frederick Marryat, or the formidable Harriet Martineau, travelled primarily as tourists and wrote up their experiences and observations for publication when they returned home. The captains were staunch Tories, and their books were highly critical of the new democracy; Miss Martineau, a proselytizing political economist (Dickens later described her as "grimly bent on the enlightenment of mankind") who warmly espoused the cause of abolition, saw the American people as "a great embryo poet: now moody, now wild, but bringing out results of absolute good sense."[2] But, whatever the viewpoint adopted, travel books about its onetime col-

---

1. Marc Pachter, introduction in *Abroad in America: Visitors to the New Nation 1776–1914*, ed. M. Pachter and F. Wein (Addison-Wesley Publishing Co. in association with the National Portrait Gallery, Smithsonian Institution, 1976), p. xiii.
2. *Society in America* (1837). Quoted by Marghanita Laski in her essay on Harriet Martineau in *Abroad in America*, p. 63.

*Frances Trollope,
from a portrait by
Auguste Hervieu*

ony sold like the hottest of cakes in Britain and were even more eagerly read, in pirated editions, in America itself. None of them caused a greater sensation, though, than Frances Trollope's *Domestic Manners of the Americans* (1832), which racily portrayed the Americans as a set of gross, greedy boors, utterly lacking in culture and refinement, arrogant and unhygienic, creators of a society of "jarring tumult and universal degradation." Her asperity can no doubt be largely attributed both to the ludicrous failure of her imprudent husband's schemes for making a fortune through the emporium she went out to set up in Cincinnati and to the subsequent discomfort of having to keep herself and several children afloat for a couple of years in an uncongenial country on very little money. But her Tory prejudices would have ensured her finding little to praise in the young republic even if the income from Trollope's bazaar had equalled the lavishness of its Moorish-Grecian-Gothic architecture.

Her book made "Dame Trollope" the best-hated woman in America[3] but made her fortune in England. Dickens joked about it in *Pick-*

---

3. Her name became a term of reproach to be shouted at anyone committing a social solecism.

wick Papers,[4] but a few years later we find him solemnly reproving another hostile English anatomiser of America for dedicating his book to the Tory premier, Sir Robert Peel:

> . . . your dedication like Mrs. Trolloppe's [*sic*] preface seems to denote a foregone conclusion. . . . My notion is that in going to a New World one must for the time utterly forget, and put out of sight the Old one and bring none of its customs or observance into the comparison – Or if you do compare remember how much brutality you may see (if you choose) in the common streets and public places of London.[5]

By the time he wrote this, in October 1841, Dickens was preparing to visit America himself. For years he had been looking forward to the event. "I shall be glad to hear," he had written to the Philadelphia publishers Lea and Blanchard in July 1838, "that Nicholas [Nickleby] is in favor with our American friends (whom I long to see)." A month later he had expressed his readiness to write for some American journals, but not until he was actually in the States because then, he said, he would be "more independent and free, which will be more in keeping." "Independent and free" – that was how he imagined the American nation – and it was a vision that brought a glow to his Radical heart. In 1840 he told C. E. Lester, a New York journalist who called on him in London, that "nothing could be more gratifying to him than to receive demonstrations of regard from American readers." "American praise," Lester reports him as saying, "is the best praise in the world for it is *sincere*," whereas most British reviews were written "under the influence of some personal feeling."[6] It seems that he was not above teasing his American admirer, however. When Lester apol-

---

4. In chapter 45 Tony Weller hastily outlines to Sam an ingenious plan for smuggling Mr. Pickwick out of prison in a hollow piano. He goes on: "Have a passage ready taken for 'Merriker. The 'Merrikin gov'ment will never give him up, ven they find as he's got money to spend, Sammy. Let the gov'nor stop there till Mrs. Bardell's dead, or Mr. Dodson and Fogg's hung . . . and then let him come back and write a book about the 'Merrikins as'll pay all his expenses and more, if he blows 'em up enough."

5. Letter to Andrew Bell, author of *Men and Things in America* (1838). See *The Pilgrim Edition of the Letters of Charles Dickens*, ed. Madeline House and Graham Storey (Oxford: Clarendon Press, 1969), vol. 2, p. 402. In subsequent notes this edition is referred to as *Pilgrim*.

6. C. E. Lester, *The Glory and Shame of England* (1841), vol. 2, p. 5. This book should have helped comfort Americans still smarting from Mrs Trollope: "When I stepped on my native soil again," Lester writes in his dedication (to Washington Irving), "my eyes had been so wearied with the sight of oppression and suffering, that I felt from my heart I could embrace every green hill-top of our own free land – I thanked God I was an American."

The SS Britannia. *Engraving after a painting by Dickens' friend Clarkson Stanfield*

ogized for asking so many questions Dickens told him to ask as many as he pleased, saying, Lester solemnly records, "as an American it is one of your *inalienable rights* to ask questions; and this, I fancy, is the reason why Yankees are so intelligent" (the extreme inquisitiveness of New Englanders was a stock joke in Victorian Britain).[7] Generally, however, Dickens made in all sincerity the kind of noises Americans wanted, and expected, to hear from one who "was almost universally regarded by them as a kind of embodied protest against what was believed to be worst in the institutions of England."[8] Thanking a Tennessee postmaster for a fan letter in February 1841, for example, he wrote, "your expressions of affectionate remembrances and approval, sounding from the green forests on the banks of the Mississippi, sink deeper in my heart and gratify it more than all the honorary distinctions that all the courts in Europe could confer."[9]

By the autumn of 1841, Dickens was nearing the end of writing *Barnaby Rudge*. He had been writing nonstop for five years. Mr. Pickwick and Sam Weller, Oliver and Nancy, Smike and Crummles, Little Nell and Dick Swiveller, Dolly Varden and Barnaby Rudge had all helped tighten his grip upon the heartstrings (and the funny bones) of both his English and his American public. Now he wanted a sabbatical. "Haunted by visions of America, night and day," he proposed to Chapman and Hall, his publishers, that he should "run over" there early in the next year and return, "after four or five months," with material for "a One Volume book." It was a travel book he had in mind, not a novel: "I don't go with any idea of pressing the Americans into my service," he told Macvey Napier. "In my next fiction, and in all others I hope, I shall stand staunchly by John [Bull]."[10] Chapman and Hall, anticipating yet another golden egg, warmly welcomed the plan, and his wife Catherine's tearful opposition to the idea of so long a separation from their home and children (for he wished her to accompany him) was soon overcome. Undaunted even by that grandest of *grandes dames*, Lady Holland, who asked him, "Why cannot you go down to Bristol and see some of the

---

7. Dickens' New England skipper, Captain Jorgan, in his 1860 Christmas story, "A Message from the Sea," is made to say, "I was raised on question-asking ground, where the babies as soon as ever they come into the world, inquire of their mothers, 'Neow, how old may *you* be, and wa'at air you a goin' to name me?' – which is a fact."

8. John Forster, *The Life of Dickens*, ed. J. W. T. Ley (London: Cecil Palmer, 1928), p. 209. Hereafter cited as Forster.

9. *Pilgrim*, vol. 2, p. 218. What Dickens felt when he eventually found himself on the Mississippi was rather different. See extract 38.

10. *Pilgrim*, vol. 2, p. 405.

Dickens' state-
room on the
Britannia

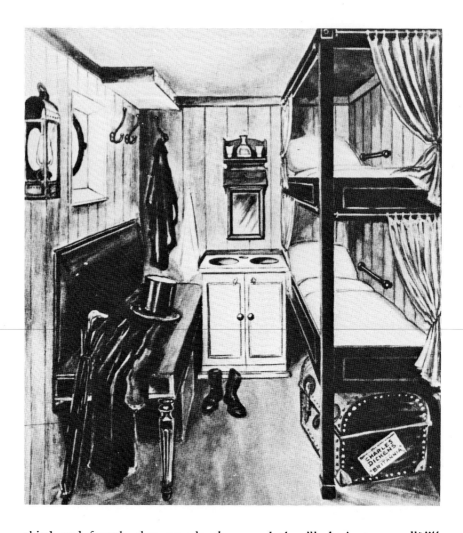

third and fourth class people there and they'll do just as well?"[11]
Dickens was soon involved in frenetic preparations for departure on
the steamship *Britannia*, due to sail from Liverpool on January 4. His
American correspondents had excited him with visions of the spectac-
ular reception he would get: "Washington Irving writes me that if I
went, it would be such a triumph from one end of the States to the
other, as was never known in any Nation."[12] He had already had a
taste of this sort of thing the previous June, when he had been fêted
in Edinburgh and given the Freedom of the City, and he would hardly have been human had he not looked forward to a lavish second

11. Quoted by Dame Una Pope-Hennessy in her *Charles Dickens* (Pelican
Books Edition, 1970), p. 221.
12. *Pilgrim*, vol. 2, p. 383.

*Dickens on board
the* Britannia.
*Sketched by Pierre
Morand*

helping across the water. But a genuine fascination with the country itself, with its political and social achievements and its physical grandeur, was the real spur that pricked the sides of his intent: "I cannot describe to you," he wrote to Lewis Gaylord Clark, editor of the New York *Knickerbocker Magazine*, "the glow into which I rise, when I think of the wonders that await us, and all the interest I am sure I shall have in your mighty land."[13]

What American expectations of Dickens were is well indicated by a leading article published during his visit in *The United States Magazine and Democratic Review* for April 1842. Who, asks the writer,

> is this young stranger, about whose path we crowd with so warm and eager a homage of our hearts – towards whom our souls thus yearn so kindly, as to some dear friend or brother whom we have long loved, though never seen – whom we are so anxious to clasp hand to hand, and to meet in that silent sympathy which passes between men like the transit of an electric spark when their eyes meet – who is he?

The answer (delivered at some length) is that he is not a soldier "crowned with all the crimsoned laurels of war," nor is he "either aristocrat or millionaire":

> As to his purse, he has to fill it from time to time by a draft on his wits, like the poorest scribbler of the tribe; and as to rank, we are rejoiced that there is no other nobility about him than the universal title of simple and glorious manhood. He is neither Prince nor Lord – but there is neither Prince nor Lord in Christendom to whom we should have awarded the ovation of such a reception.

What makes him a hero for the Americans, continues the writer, is "the accordance of the spirit generally pervading his writings with the democratic genius now everywhere rapidly developing itself as the principle of that new civilization, whose dawn is just brightening upon the world." Wellington and Peel are warned that they would be wise to lock Dickens up on his return from a country "where his popular tendencies are not likely to be weakened," for his writings will "hasten on the great crisis of the English Revolution (speed the hour!) far more effectively than any of the open assaults of Radicalism or Chartism": "The great idea they all assert is that idea of human equality, under the influence of the progress of which the

13. *Pilgrim*, vol. 2, p. 445.

regal palaces and baronial castles of the whole world are crumbling and destined to crumble to ruin."[14]

America, it seems, expected a sort of young messiah of democracy whilst Dickens, for his part, expected to behold the promised land. Mutual disillusion was inevitable and would certainly have come more swiftly if the SS *Britannia* had sailed, like the *Screw* in *Martin Chuzzlewit*, into New York rather than Boston. For Anglophile Boston (soon to be nicknamed "Boz-town" by the jealous New Yorkers) managed, more or less, to live up even to Dickens' expectations and was duly celebrated in *American Notes* (see extract 28). It was, Dickens said later, what he would have liked the whole United States to be and, Forster significantly tells us, he was fond of comparing it to Edinburgh "as Edinburgh was in the days when several dear friends of his own still lived there."[15]

It was certainly an exhilarating arrival for Dickens, that January Saturday evening in Boston harbour. He was saluted from the shore by a press reception committee, and when his wife "called his attention to the inadequacy of his travelling costume for the occasion," he replied, "Never mind that, dear, we are on the other side now."[16] The tiresome petty formalities of England could be forgotten in the land of liberty. Dickens and his party were escorted in triumph to their hotel, and he soon emerged with a friend he had made on the voyage, the young Earl of Mulgrave, for a joyous moonlight reconnaissance of the snow-covered streets of the city. James Fields, a young admirer who became one of Dickens' closest American friends, followed them and later recalled, "Dickens kept up one continual shout of uproarious laughter as he went rapidly forward, reading the signs on the shops and observing the architecture of the new country into which he had dropped as from the clouds."[17]

Dickens spent two packed weeks in Boston, fêted in theatres, at a public ball, at private dinner and breakfast parties, and in the streets everywhere he went. He visited the state capitol, the courthouse, an

---

14. There is, according to this eulogist, "one striking defect" in Dickens' work, however: the "atrocious exaggeration of his bad characters." Nell "needs no such foil to the sweet radiance of her halo" as the monstrous Quilp. Noah Claypole and his oysters seem to distress the writer even more. "But," he sighs, "Mr. Dickens is 'a privileged character', and we suppose we must put up with his eccentricities . . ."

15. Forster, p. 766.

16. Pierre Morand, a fellow passenger of Dickens' on the SS *Britannia*; quoted in *The Dickensian*, vol. 15 (1919), p. 173.

17. James T. Fields, *Yesterdays with Authors* (Boston: Houghton Mifflin & Co., 1887), p. 128 f.

Dickens in Boston,
January 1842.
Sketched by Pierre
Morand

Professor Felton,
"not at all starry
or stripey"

institute for the blind, a factory (see extract 46), a seamen's chapel,
and Harvard University. He hired a secretary to help cope with the
flood of correspondence which poured into his hotel rooms, he had
his portrait painted and his bust sculpted, he received an endless stream
of visitors, distinguished and undistinguished, and he established warm
friendships with a number of people, among them Longfellow and a
jovial, oyster-loving professor of Greek at Harvard, C. C. Felton, "not
at all starry *or* stripey,"[18] who became one of his best-loved American
friends. The culmination was a great public dinner, given in his honour by the "Young Men of Boston" on February 1. In his speech on
that occasion Dickens said he had "dreamed by day and night, for
years, of setting foot upon this shore, and breathing this pure air."
Even if he had come there as an unknown, he continued, he would
"have come with all my sympathies clustering as richly about this land
and people – with all my sense of justice as keenly alive to their high
claims on every man who loves God's image."[19]

18. Dickens so described Felton in 1853. See *Letters of Charles Dickens*, ed.
W. Dexter (Bloomsbury: Nonesuch Press, 1938), vol. 2, p. 460. This edition
of Dickens' correspondence is hereafter referred to as Nonesuch *Letters*.

19. *The Speeches of Charles Dickens*, ed. K. J. Fielding (Oxford: Clarendon
Press, 1960), p. 19.

He was exhausted but triumphant. "There never was a King or Emperor upon the Earth, so cheered, and followed by crowds, and entertained in Public at splendid balls and dinners, and waited on by public bodies and deputations of all kinds," he wrote to one of his English friends.[20] All this clearly had its inconvenient side, as we learn from a letter written to the American historian J. L. Motley by Mrs. Motley:

> Somebody told me that the other evening, when he was obliged to stay at home from perfect exhaustion of body and mind, that a man inquired for him at the Tremont House, and, in spite of Dickens's repeated refusals to see him, contrived to make his way into his parlour, where the poor man was extended on the sofa; he remained an hour and then requested Mr. D. to allow him to bring up his wife, who was waiting below. Dickens told him he really must excuse him, he was too ill to remain up any longer, and went to his room and threw himself on the bed. In spite of this, the man brought up his wife and passed another hour with Mrs. Dickens. Did you ever hear anything so disgusting? The women – not the common people, for that you could excuse – float round him in the streets, wait for him at corners, and Alexander's room [where Dickens' portrait was being painted] is crammed every day with girls and women who call themselves ladies, to see him when he comes out of the studio. The other day he was absolutely obliged to force himself through the crowd, and one woman stepped before him and said to him: 'Mr. Dickens, will you be kind enough to walk entirely round the room, so that we can all have a look at you?' This is one of the million things which I could tell you which make me feel sometimes as if I should cry with mortification.[21]

But Dickens himself seems to have forgiven the Bostonians everything. They are, he wrote to the actor W. C. Macready on January 31, "as delicate, as considerate, as careful of giving the least offence, as the best Englishmen I ever saw. – I like their behaviour to Ladies infinitely better than that of my own countrymen; and their Institutions I reverence, love, and honor."[22]

This mood seems to have been sustained until after he had been a few days in New York, to which he travelled from Boston via Worcester, Springfield, Hartford (where he spoke at another public banquet in his honour), and New Haven. New York, Dickens found,

---

20. *Pilgrim*, vol. 3, p. 43.

21. *J. L. Motley and his Family*, ed. S. and H. St. John Mildmay (1910), p. 25.

22. *Pilgrim*, vol. 3, p. 44.

*The great Boz Ball,
14 February 1842*

was determined to outdo Boston in fêting him. A committee of prominent citizens had been formed to organise a grand soirée, which came
to be called "the Boz Ball," at the Park Theatre on February 14.
Thousands of people attended, paying five dollars a head. The theatre
was "decorated and embellished in a style of elegance far surpassing
anything of the kind ever seen in that house,"[23] the band played "God
Save the King" on Dickens' entrance and the crowd broke into "loud
demonstrations of applause," a series of *tableaux vivants* depicting
scenes and characters from his books was presented, the pit had been
boarded over to form a huge dance floor, and a lavish buffet supper[24]
was served in an upstairs saloon. The affair was derided by some sections of the press (especially, of course, the Boston papers)[25] and by
some private individuals as ludicrously farfetched and tasteless, but
Dickens himself seems to have enjoyed "this extraordinary festival,"
as he called it. A few days later he was honoured again, in a more
conventional way, at a public dinner chaired by Washington Irving
(with whom he had established a thriving, and very genuine, mutual
admiration society).

23. Report in a New York paper, *The Spirit of the Times*, 19 February
1842. Reprinted in *The Dickensian*, vol. 4 (1908), pp. 204–206.

24. "The bill of fare for supper, is, in its amount and extent, quite a
curiosity," Dickens wrote to Forster. See illus., pp. 16–17.

25. The *Boston Transcript* ironically enquired why the managers of the
Park Theatre did not "engage Mr. Dickens for a few evenings to show him-
self on the stage!" and the *Boston Post* called the ball "a ridiculous burlesque –
converting an act of courtesy to a private gentleman into a raree show."
Quoted by Paul B. Davies in "Dickens and the American Press, 1842,"
Dickens Studies, vol. 4 (1968), p. 75.

The Park Theatre, New York, where the Boz Ball was held

Ladies ticket of admission to the Boz Ball

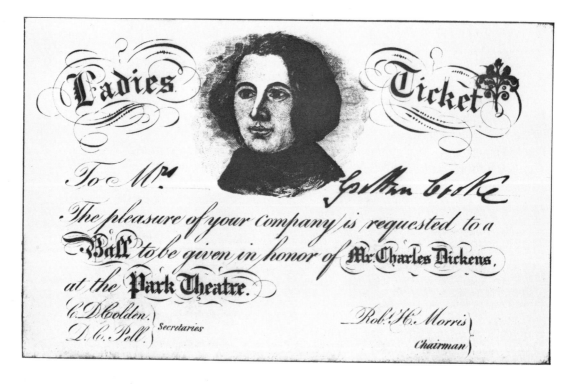

Partial *program of
the* tableaux vi-
vants *for the Boz
Ball*

TABLEAUX VIVANS.

BOZ BALL.

February 14th, 1842.

ORDER OF THE DANCES AND TABLEAUX VIVANS.

1.—GRAND MARCH.

2.--TABLEAU VIVANT--"Mrs. Leo Hunter's dress *déjeûné.*"

" ' Is it possible that I have really the gratification of beholding Mr.
Pickwick himself?" ejaculated Mrs. Leo Hunter. 'No other,
ma'am,' replied Mr. Pickwick, bowing very low. ' Permit me to
introduce my friends—Mr. Tupman—Mr. Winkle—Mr. Snodgrass—to the authoress of the ' expiring frog.' "—*Pickwick Papers.*

3.—AMELIE QUADRILLE.

**4.—TABLEAU VIVANT—" The middle-aged lady in the
double-bedded room."**

"The only way in which Mr. Pickwick could catch a glimpse of his
mysterious visiter, with the least danger of being seen himself, was
by creeping on to a bed, and peeping out from between the curtains
on the opposite side. To this manœuvre he accordingly resorted.—
Keeping the curtains carefully closed with his hand, so that nothing
more of him could be seen than his face and night-cap, and putting on his spectacles, he mustered up courage, and looked out.—
Mr. Pickwick almost fainted with horror and dismay. Standing before the dressing-glass, was a middle-aged lady in yellow curl-papers,
busily engaged in brushing what ladies call their ' back hair.' It was
quite clear that she contemplated remaining there for the night; for
she brought a rush-light and shade with her, which, with praisewor-
thy precaution against fire, she had stationed in a basin on the floor,
where it was glimmering away, like a gigantic lighthouse in a particularly small piece of water.'

5.—QUADRILLE WALTZ—selections.

**6.—TABLEAU VIVANT--" Mrs. Bardell faints in Mr. Pick-
wick's arms."**

" ' Oh, you kind, good, playful dear,' said Mrs. Bardell, and without
more ado she rose from her chair and flung her arms round Mr. Pickwick's neck, with a cataract of tears and a chorus of sobs. ' Bless
my soul!' cried the astonished Mr. Pickwick. ' Mrs. Bardell, my
good woman—dear me—what a situation—pray, consider—Mrs.
Bardell, don't—if any body should come!—' —' Oh! let them
come,' exclaimed Mrs. Bardell, frantically ; ' I'll never leave you—
dear, kind, good soul.' And with these words, Mrs. Bardell clung the
tighter. ' Mercy upon me,' said Mr. Pickwick, struggling violently ;
' I hear somebody coming up the stairs. Don't—don't, there's a good
creature don't !' But entreaty and remonstrance were alike unavailing ;
for Mrs. Bardell had fainted in Mr. Pickwick's arms ; and before he
could gain time to deposit her in a chair, Master Bardell entered
the room, ushering in Mr. Tupman, Mr. Winkle and Mr. Snodgrass."

Conclusion of a letter from Dickens to his friend Daniel Maclise, dated 27 February 1842, with pasted-on cuttings from newspaper reports of the Boz Ball

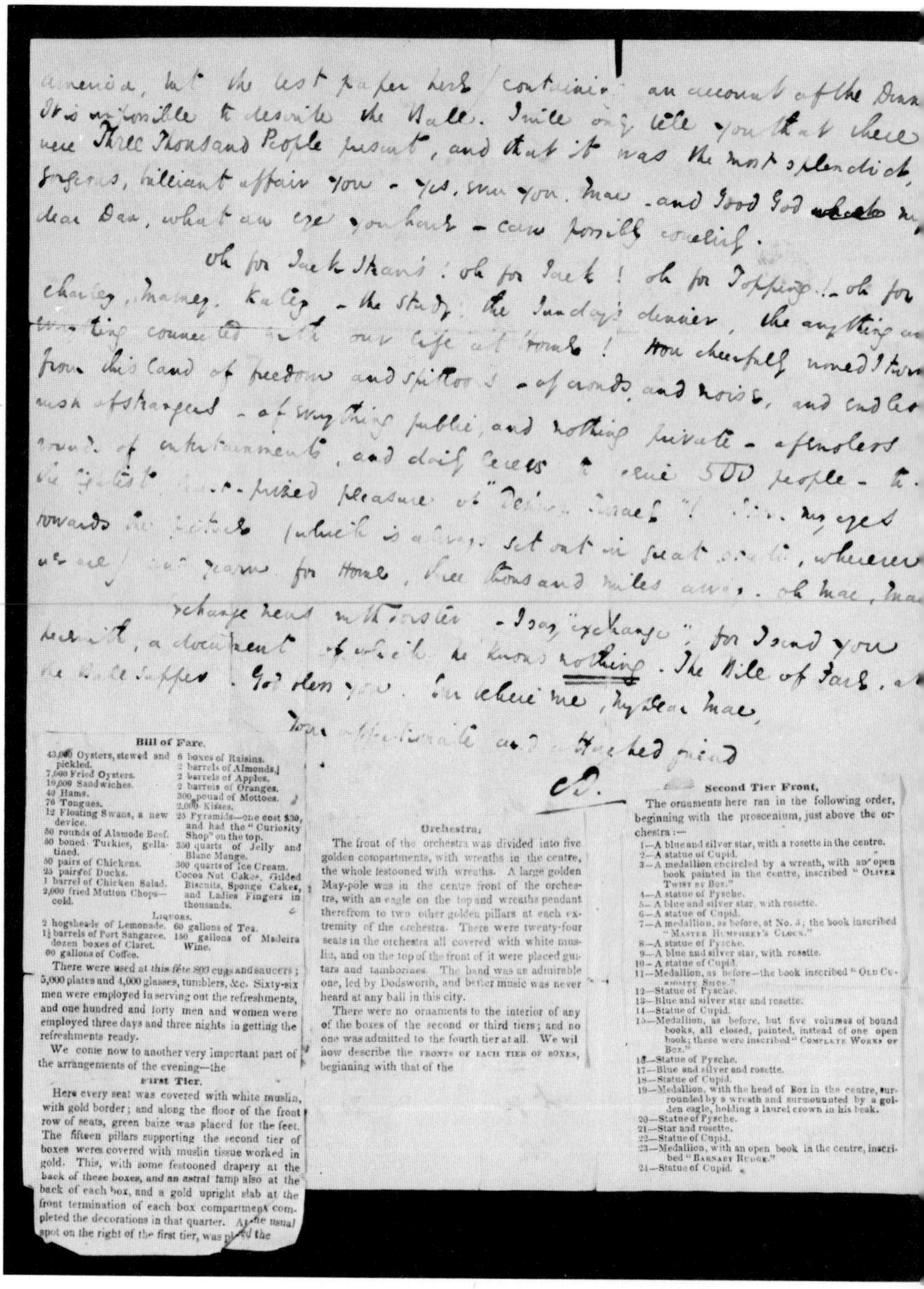

Bill of Fare.

43,000 Oysters, stewed and pickled.
7,000 Fried Oysters.
10,000 Sandwiches.
40 Hams.
76 Tongues.
12 Floating Swans, a new device.
50 rounds of Alamode Beef.
50 boned Turkies, gellatined.
50 pairs of Chickens.
25 pairs of Ducks.
1 barrel of Chicken Salad.
2,000 fried Mutton Chops—cold.
6 boxes of Raisins.
2 barrels of Almonds.
2 barrels of Apples.
2 barrels of Oranges.
300 pound of Mottoes.
2,000 Kisses.
25 Pyramids—one cost $30, and had the "Curiosity Shop" on the top.
350 quarts of Jelly and Blanc Mange.
300 quarts of Ice Cream.
Cocoa Nut Cakes, Gilded Biscuits, Sponge Cakes, and Ladies Fingers in thousands.

LIQUORS.

2 hogsheads of Lemonade.
1½ barrels of Port Sangaree.
dozen boxes of Claret.
00 gallons of Coffee.
60 gallons of Tea.
150 gallons of Madeira Wine.

There were used at this fête 800 cups and saucers; 5,000 plates and 4,000 glasses, tumblers, &c. Sixty-six men were employed in serving out the refreshments, and one hundred and forty men and women were employed three days and three nights in getting the refreshments ready.

We come now to another very important part of the arrangements of the evening—the

First Tier.

Here every seat was covered with white muslin, with gold border; and along the floor of the front row of seats, green baize was placed for the feet. The fifteen pillars supporting the second tier of boxes were covered with muslin tissue worked in gold. This, with some festooned drapery at the back of these boxes, and an astral lamp also at the back of each box, and a gold upright slab at the front termination of each box compartment completed the decorations in that quarter. At the usual spot on the right of the first tier, was placed the

Orchestra.

The front of the orchestra was divided into five golden compartments, with wreaths in the centre, the whole festooned with wreaths. A large golden May-pole was in the centre front of the orchestra, with an eagle on the top and wreaths pendant therefrom to two other golden pillars at each extremity of the orchestra. There were twenty-four seats in the orchestra all covered with white muslin, and on the top of the front of it were placed guitars and tamborines. The band was an admirable one, led by Dodsworth, and better music was never heard at any ball in this city.

There were no ornaments to the interior of any of the boxes of the second or third tiers; and no one was admitted to the fourth tier at all. We wil now describe the FRONTS OF EACH TIER OF BOXES, begiuning with that of the

Second Tier Front.

The ornaments here ran in the following order, beginning with the proscenium, just above the orchestra:—

1—A blue and silver star, with a rosette in the centre.
2—A statue of Cupid.
3—A medallion encircled by a wreath, with an open book painted in the centre, inscribed "OLIVER TWIST BY BOZ."
4—A statue of Pysche.
5—A blue and silver star, with rosette.
6—A statue of Cupid.
7—A medallion, as before, at No. 3; the book inscribed "MASTER HUMPHREY'S CLOCK."
8—A statue of Pysche.
9—A blue and silver star, with rosette.
10—A statue of Cupid.
11—Medallion, as before—the book inscribed "OLD CURIOSITY SHOP."
12—Statue of Pysche.
13—Blue and silver star and rosette.
14—Statue of Cupid.
15—Medallion, as before, but five volumes of bound books, all closed, painted, instead of one open book; these were inscribed "COMPLETE WORKS OF BOZ."
16—Statue of Pysche.
17—Blue and silver and rosette.
18—Statue of Cupid.
19—Medallion, with the head of Boz in the centre, surrounded by a wreath and surmounted by a golden eagle, holding a laurel crown in his beak.
20—Statue of Pysche.
21—Star and rosette.
22—Statue of Cupid.
23—Medallion, with an open book in the centre, inscribed "BARNABY RUDGE."
24—Statue of Cupid.

25—Star and rosette.
26—Statue of Psyche.
27—Medallion and book, inscribed "PICKWICK PAPERS."
28—Statue of Cupid.
29—Star and rosette.
30—Statue of Psyche.
31—Medallion and book, inscribed "NICHOLAS NICKLEBY."
32—Statue of Cupid.
33—Blue and silver star and rosette.

This, with a continuous wreath festooned all round, completed the ornaments round the front of the first tier from proscenium to proscenium pillar.

Round the front of the Third Tier

were placed all the shields of the twenty-six States in regular order, beginning at the oldest in the with festoons of flowers continued all round the boxes front, and over each shield were English and American flags crossed.

In the Front of the Fourth Tier

Were placed statues and portraits in the following order,—beginning with the centre :—

Full length figure of Washington.
Head of John Adams.
Head of Madison.
Head of Monroe.
Head of Jefferson.
Arms of the States.
A Star.
Statue of Liberty.

Full length figure of Jefferson.
Head of Washington.
Head of John Quincey Adams.
Head of Jackson.
Arms of the States.
A Star.
Statue of Justice.

Over each of these were placed the English and American ensigns crossed; and between them were placed statues of Apollo and the nine muses; the whole decorated with wreaths and continuous festoons of flowers.

Boxes of the Second Tier.

To this, we must add, that every one of the sixteen boxes in the tier were fitted up with red striped drapery curtains to represent tents, each curtain having a blue ground in the corner with 26 stars thereon.

The Proscenium.

On the proscenium the pillars were covered with striped bunting, and above them were four silk banners with appropriate devices; portraits of Boz on two of them.

The Dome.

The entire dome over the pit was covered with red, white, and blue bunting, radiating from a large golden star in the centre; and diverging at the stage side in curved festoons, till it covered all the ceiling up to the proscenium. Altogether 7,000 yards of bunting were used in the decorations; which all, from first to last, cost about $2,500; although much was only hired for the occasion.

Chandeliers, &c.

In the centre of the audience part of the house, over the pit, were two splendid golden chandeliers with sixty variegated wax candles therein. At the main box entrance, where the green baize reached the stage, were two golden pillars, supporting golden candelabras, with twelve variegated wax lights in each. These, with the astral lamps at the back of the boxes of the first tier, projecting from brackets, and six golden astral lamps hanging from golden brackets on the proscenium pillars, with the usual number of sixteen chandelier gas lights of four burners each, in front of each tier of boxes, formed the whole of the lights in front of the proscenium. The whole of these were from the establishment of Stoutenburgh & Cox, Bro

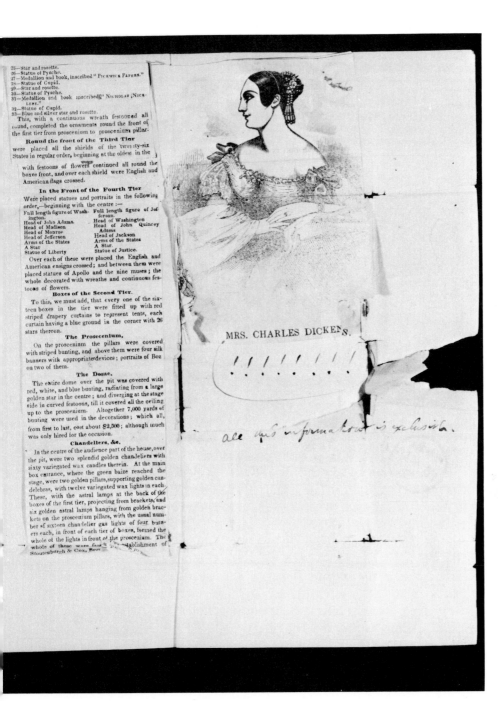

MRS. CHARLES DICKENS.

all this information is exclusive

Washington Irving

But it is clear that his feelings toward America underwent a great change about this time. The editors of the *Pilgrim Edition* of his letters pinpoint this reaction to the three days (February 15–17) when illness confined him to his hotel room and he was "able to read and reflect on reports and editorials in the newspapers."[26] He found himself savagely attacked for daring to advocate the cause of international copyright in his speeches at Boston and Hartford. Of course, the very newspapers that were attacking him, such as the "mammoth" *New World*, were the greatest profiteers from the wholesale piracy of his works that was made possible by the absence of any copyright agreement between England and America. Insult was heaped on injury. "Some of the vagabonds," he wrote to Forster, "take great credit to themselves (grant us patience!) for having made me popular by publishing my books in newspapers: as if there were no England, no Scotland, no Germany, no place but America in the whole world."[27] He was further incensed by the accusation that his whole object in coming to the States was

26. *Pilgrim*, vol. 3, p. x.   27. Forster, p. 220.

simply and sordidly to campaign for international copyright. With characteristic vehemence, he wrote on February 22 to his friend Jonathan Chapman, mayor of Boston, "I vow to Heaven that the scorn and indignation I have felt under this unmanly and ungenerous treatment has been to me an amount of agony such as I never experienced since my birth."[28] Even the traumatic blacking factory of his childhood palled, it would seem, in the comparison.

Nor did the sneering, patronising tone of much of the newspaper comment on his public behaviour do anything to assuage his wrath, as we can see from extract 3 below (one would like to have had Lady Holland's comment on the assertion that "Dickens was never in such society in England as he has seen in New York"). From this time date Dickens' violent animosity toward the all too "independent and free" American press and his conviction that it was a veritable cancer in the body politic of the young nation. Extracts 42 and 55 represent some of his more vigorous onslaughts on the hated institution. The press proved itself as formidable an opponent as Spenser's Blatant Beast, resorting, as we shall see, to downright forgery as well as slanderous misrepresentation, and the battle continued merrily for many years after Dickens' 1842 visit. Reconcilement did not come until 1868, when Dickens agreed to attend a press banquet in his honour in New York and chose this platform to make his *amende honorable* to the American nation (see extract 88).

The horrific Tombs prison in New York and the equally horrific lunatic asylum on Long Island, the savage squalor of the Five Points, the roaming pigs on fashionable Broadway, all combined to intensify Dickens' revulsion of feelings about America. The crowds of inquisitive sightseers were no longer exhilarating, as they had been in Boston, but wearisome and grossly intrusive. The extracts in the first section of this anthology show that as Dickens penetrated deeper into the country after leaving New York he became more and more disgusted and offended by the Americans' table manners, their fondness for spitting in public, their endless talk about money, their boastful patriotism, their condonement of violence in public life, and their worship of "smartness" (shrewd and successful swindling). In Philadelphia he was filled with horror by the high-minded inhumanity of the solitary-confinement prison system, a horror which, years later, he turned to great imaginative account in his portrayal of the ruined Dr. Manette in *A Tale of Two Cities*. In Washington he saw "Dishonest Faction in its most depraved and most unblushing form" staring out from every corner of the House of Representatives' assembly hall. In Vir-

---

28. *Pilgrim*, vol. 3, p. 77. Compare extract 4.

Niagara from "the English side"

ginia he was appalled by his glimpse of slavery and its defenders. Indeed, this was not the republic of his imagination, not the republic he had come to see.[29] Even the very landscape became a nightmare as he journeyed down the Mississippi or jolted over corduroy roads in Ohio. Niagara Falls alone, like Boston, lived up to his expectations, indeed surpassed them, but especially when viewed from "the English side."

II

Thankfully back in England at the end of June 1842, Dickens set to work on the travel book promised to his publishers. He had made no public references to this projected work whilst in America nor, apparently, did he even mention it to his private friends there, but that he would certainly write such a book, following the well-established precedent created by earlier British visitors, was confidently anticipated by his recent hosts. Speculation about it was rife, and many feared that it was bound to pass an unfavourable verdict on their country.[30] If they could have seen a letter written by Mary Shelley to

29. See extract 13.

30. The *Pilgrim* editors quote an English emigrant as saying that the Americans were "writhing 'under the anticipated malediction of Boz'" (*Pilgrim*, vol. 3, p. xii).

Claire Clairmont they would have felt still more anxious: "Charles Dickens has just come home in a state of violent dislike of the Americans – and means to devour them in his next work – he says they are so frightfully dishonest."[31] As it was, the American press was warned of the sort of treatment they might expect by the appearance in the British press in July of a circular from Dickens on the subject of international copyright. In it he observed:

> The persons who exert themselves to mislead the American public on this question; to put down its discussion; and to suppress and distort the truth, in reference to it, in every possible way; are (as you may easily suppose) those who have a strong interest in the existing system of piracy and plunder; inasmuch as, so long as it continues, they can gain a very comfortable living out of the brains of other men while they would find it very difficult to earn bread by the exercise of their own. These are the editors and proprietors of newspapers almost exclusively devoted to the republication of popular English works. They are for the most part, men of very low attainments, and of more than indifferent reputation . . .[32]

This paragraph was reproduced in various American papers and in some was embellished with further paragraphs invented by an ingenious American journalist but published as though also written by Dickens. These forged paragraphs offensively castigated the Americans for their "worship of pelf" and their "meanness," complained of their dinners and balls "forced upon me, many times to the serious inconvenience of myself and my party," and declared that "the total difference between our good old English customs, and the awkwardness, the uncouth manners, and the unmitigated selfishness which meet you everywhere in America, made my journey one of a good deal of annoyance."[33] Dickens was naturally outraged by this brazen fraud but disdained to publish any repudiation of it. He had his revenge later, though, in chapter 16 of *Martin Chuzzlewit*, where Martin, after inspecting a copy of the *New York Rowdy Journal*, hesitantly asks its editor, Colonel Diver,[34] whether the paper ever deals in "forged letters . . . solemnly purporting to have been written at recent periods by living men." Far from being abashed, the colonel cheerfully admits

---

31. Quoted by R. B. Heilman in his "The New World in Charles Dickens's Writings," *The Trollopian*, vol. 1 (1946), p. 30.

32. *Pilgrim*, vol. 3, p. 258 f.

33. For a full text of the forgery see *Pilgrim*, vol. 3, pp. 625–627.

34. "Diver" was eighteenth-century slang for pickpocket (cf. Jenny Diver in *The Beggar's Opera*).

the fact and boasts that the paper sells hugely in consequence. "We are a smart people here, and can appreciate smartness," he tells the wondering Martin.

All this while Dickens was working away at his travel book, which he decided to call *American Notes for General Circulation*. That the title itself was intended to carry on his war against the piratical American press is clear from the motto he proposed to print on the book's title page:

> In reply to a question from the Bench, the Solicitor for the Bank observed, that this kind of notes circulated the most extensively, in those parts of the world where they were stolen or forged. – *Old Bailey Report*.[35]

Forster dissuaded him from making such an obvious gesture of provocation at the "vagabonds" (Dickens' usual term for American journalists and editors), but the title remained. Forster also managed to dissuade him from publishing a prefatory chapter entitled "Introductory and Necessary to be Read," because "its proper self-assertion" might be mistaken for "an apprehension of hostile judgments which he was anxious to deprecate or avoid."[36] It is a pity Dickens yielded to Forster over this, since the chapter makes clear what sort of book *American Notes* is intended to be and what it is not. It is not to be statistical or political, nor will it describe individuals met by Dickens or give any account of his own personal reception in America. The reason for this last omission, Dickens says, is

> not because I am, or ever was, insensible to that spontaneous effusion of affection and generosity of heart, in a most affectionate and generous-hearted people; but because I conceive that it would ill become me to flourish matter necessarily involving so much of my own praises, in the eyes of my unhappy readers.

He realises, he says, that he will not please that "numerous class of well-intentioned persons prone to be dissatisfied with all accounts of the Republic whose citizens they are, which are not couched in terms of exalted and extravagant praise," and he knows also that "they who will be aptest to detect malice, ill-will and all uncharitableness" in the book will be "certain native journalists, veracious and gentlemanly, who were at great pains to prove to me . . . during my stay there, that

---

35. Forster, p. 283.
36. Forster, p. 284. Dickens agreed to suppress this introduction only on the condition that Forster should see that it was published "when a more fitting time should come." It was accordingly printed in Forster, pp. 284–286.

[my] welcome was utterly worthless." To the question, "If you have been in any respect disappointed in America, and are assured beforehand that the expression of your disappointment will give offence to any class, why do you write at all?" he answers:

> I went there expecting greater things than I found, and resolved as far as in me lay to do justice to the country, at the expense of any (in my view) mistaken or prejudiced statements that might have been made to its disparagement. Coming home with a corrected and sobered judgment, I consider myself no less bound to do justice to what, according to my best means of judgment, I found to be the truth.

Grand as this sounds, it is not perhaps altogether convincing. Dickens was committed to making a book of his travels, whatever happened to him in America, and his reaching for such sounding clichés as "as far as in me lay" betrays a certain uneasiness, I think. However, there can be little doubt that this preface, if published, would have helped the eager first readers of *American Notes*, on both sides of the Atlantic, arrive at a fairer judgment of the work.

To the modern reader, unaware of the context of its publication, *American Notes* must seem an unlikely book to have stirred up such excitement as it did. Even most American readers today, Edgar Johnson comments, will find little in it "to rouse their ire."[37] Another modern American scholar has acclaimed Dickens as "a shrewd and thoughtful observer, especially in his account of the phases of American life which had dangerous implications," adding that "his pronouncements could easily be the text of many American critics of America today [1946]."[38] But the American press of 1842 was, like General Cyrus Choke, U.S.M., in chapter 21 of *Chuzzlewit*, "greatly heated . . . in a fit state to receive any inflammable influences." No sooner had the first copies – pirated ones, naturally – of *American Notes* gone on sale in the streets of New York than the outcry arose. The *New York Herald* pronounced Dickens' mind to be "coarse, vulgar, impudent and superficial" and his book "the essence of balderdash, reduced to

---

37. Edgar Johnson, *Charles Dickens: His Tragedy and Triumph* (New York: Simon and Schuster, 1952), vol. 1, p. 443. Professor Johnson's analysis (pp. 444–446) of the "three intertwining roots" of Dickens' hostility toward America in 1842 seems to me very just and illuminating. He distinguishes these roots as "Dickens's own limitations, the distortions inevitable in the only view of America he was given, and the actual character of the nation in the mid-nineteenth century."

38. Heilman, "The New World in Charles Dickens's Writings."

American Notes,
*with an inscription
to George Wash-
ington Putnam,
Dickens' "faithful
friend and fellow-
traveller"*

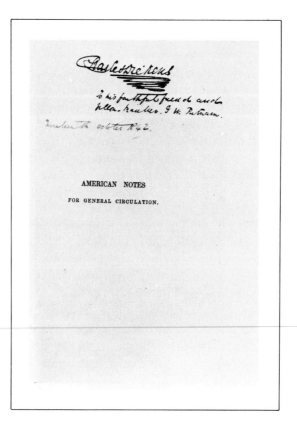

the last drop of silliness and inanity."[39] Another organ of egalitarian democracy so far forgot itself as to brand Dickens "a low-bred scullion unexpectedly advanced from the kitchen to the parlor."[40] A counterblast soon appeared in Boston. Entitled *English Notes, intended for Very Extensive Circulation!*, it was written under the pseudonym of "Quarles Quickens, Esq.,"[41] which gives some idea of the quality of its wit.

English Notes is part parody and part counterattack. In reply to Dickens' strictures on American railways "Quickens" writes:

39. Quoted by Edward Payne in "Dickens's First Look at America," *The Dickensian*, vol. 38 (1942), p. 13.

40. Newspaper clipping in the Forster Collection, Victoria and Albert Museum, quoted by Johnson, *Charles Dickens*, vol. 1, p. 442.

41. *English Notes* was for many years erroneously ascribed to Edgar Allan Poe. See *English Notes. A Rare and Unknown Work being a Reply to Charles Dickens's "American Notes,"* with critical comments by Joseph Jackson and George H. Sargent, privately published by Lewis M. Thompson (New York, 1920).

Now an English railway car is one of the most dirty, foolish and unchristian conveyances that ever disgraced any civilized age or country; instead of being large, open and airy as are ours, it is in fact but a long succession of Yankee stage coaches, (I mean the first class) opening at the side, the interior space divided by partitions with little cells, wherein when you have thrust yourself into its seclusion, you feel very much like a convict in one of our State Prisons, only not half as comfortable.

"Quickens" meets a middle-class Englishwoman, who asks him what tribe he belongs to, as she assumes all Americans must be Red Indians, and is appalled by the "half-clothed, half-fed and uneducated population" he observes in English city streets, "wallowing in the same mire that their fathers and grandfathers wallowed in before them." They are ground down by "the Juggernaut of British aristocracy," and Dickens' horrifying series of extracts from southern newspapers in his

Illustration by Alfred Crowquill to a comic song entitled "Yankee Notes for English Circulation, or Boz in A-Merry-Key." This song, by James Briton, was published by T. E. Purday, St. Paul's Churchyard, London, in 1842

chapter on slavery is counterattacked by a series of extracts from British papers about the desperate poverty of the lower classes and British-sanctioned slavery in India. The most vindictive part of the book is an open letter to "Quickens," feigned to have been published in *The Morning Post*, which brings together all those newspaper slanders and half truths that had so enraged Dickens during his time in the States:

> . . . Many circumstances connected with your visit seem to favor the impression in some minds that its object was of a mercenary character. A steam voyage across the Atlantic in mid-winter presents but few attractions for even the most hearty and robust, to say nothing of its perils! The face of this portion of our country is known to wear a somewhat gloomy aspect in the seasons of winter and spring. . . .

> . . . You set out on your voyage to this country with false impressions of the character of our institutions and the manners of our people. The whole army of *American* tourists in *England*, themselves at your elbow, and their books upon your shelves, had instilled into you the whole of that rancor and abuse which they had not dared but in part to express in their works. . . .

> . . . when you visit this country again . . . never make any allusions to the shop in your public addresses; this matter of international copyright has a strong odor. . . . And lastly, never be ungrateful for civilities which you know are honestly meant, however awkwardly expressed.

It is to be hoped that Dickens never saw a copy of this highly offensive production, but the venomous points it made were certainly all odiously familiar to him and the clamour that arose about *American Notes* no doubt made him decide to retort fiercely in *Martin Chuzzlewit*. "I do perceive a perplexingly divided and subdivided duty, in the matter of the book of travels," he had written to Forster whilst still in America. "Oh! the subliminated essence of comicality that I *could* distil, from the materials I have!"[42]

Very little indeed of this "essence of comicality" that he eventually poured into *Chuzzlewit* gets into *American Notes*. In consequence it has generally been pronounced a dull book and, certainly, any true Dickensian must prefer the much more personalised and impressionistic *Pictures from Italy*, with its "inimitable" accounts of the bizarre pageantry of Holy Week in Rome, the ludicrous Neapolitan puppet

---

42. *Pilgrim*, vol. 3, p. 211.

show, and so on. Even the "fine writing" in *Pictures*, such as the verbal panorama of "dream-like" Venice, is much better than the description of Niagara, the only truly purple patch in the *Notes*. That most insightful of all Dickens critics, G. K. Chesterton, puts his finger on a notable difference between the two travel books when he writes of Dickens' feeling a sort of "family responsibility" in inspecting America, whereas in truly foreign Italy he could just relax and be a gossiping tourist:

> Dickens is cross with America because he is worried about America; as if he were its father. He explores its industrial, legal and educational arrangements like a mother looking at the housekeeping of a married son; he makes suggestions with a certain acidity; he takes a strange pleasure in being pessimistic. He advises them to take note of how much better certain things are done in England.[43]

This "mother-in-law" tone is not characteristic of the whole of *American Notes*, however. Chapters 3, 4, and 5, dealing with Boston and New England, may be rather in this vein, but there is more praise than Chesterton's description suggests. Disapproval becomes marked in Dickens' account of New York, but something more than disapproval appears in his brief description of the Tombs prison there, "a dismal-fronted pile of bastard Egyptian, like an enchanter's palace in a melodrama." Dickens' imagination, always strongly stirred by prisons, begins to take over and is in full force in the next chapter, when he describes the system of solitary confinement practised in the Eastern penitentiary in Philadelphia. He writes about the latter with just the same powerful projection of himself into the prisoner's place as he had written about the condemned cell in Newgate in *Sketches by Boz* or was to write about the prison adjoining the Doge's Palace in *Pictures from Italy*. He imagines a man brought, hooded, to the cell in which he will be isolated for years:

> At first the man is stunned. His confinement is a hideous vision; and his old life a reality. He throws himself upon his bed, and lies there abandoned to despair. By degrees the insupportable solitude and barrenness of the place rouses him from this stupor, and when the trap in his grated door is opened, he humbly

---

43. Introduction to Everyman's Library Edition of *American Notes* (London: J. M. Dent, 1908). To his American friend, Jonathan Chapman, Dickens wrote on 15 October 1842, "I dispassionately believe that in the slow fulness of time, what I have written will have some effect in purging your community of evils which threaten its very existence" (*Pilgrim*, vol. 3, p. 346).

The Tombs prison, New York, "like an enchanter's palace in a melodrama"

begs and prays for work. "Give me some work to do, or I shall go raving mad!"

Dickens continues in this vein for ten more paragraphs, as though working out a private nightmare (as, indeed, he was), before returning to Chesterton's "mother-in-law" tone. This is some of the most powerful writing in *American Notes*, but I have not included any of it in this anthology because it seems to me to transcend the matter of America altogether. It is something that happened to Dickens in America but might have happened anywhere and, indeed, did so whenever he got near a prison, English, American, or European.

His experience in the Eastern penitentiary certainly darkens the tone of the book, however. A certain horror underlies all his subsequent descriptions. America begins to seem a series of prisons: the "unhealthy" prison of Washington, where few would live who were not "obliged to reside there"; the "dismal swamp" of the Mississippi, Dickens' Heart of Darkness, pictured as one huge Condemned Cell, "in whose baleful shade the wretched wanderers who are tempted hither, droop, and die, and lay their bones"; the stupefying "open prison" of the Looking-glass Prairie, "oppressive in its barren monotony," where the traveller would feel "little of that sense of freedom

The Eastern state penitentiary, Pennsylvania

and exhilaration which a Scottish heath inspires, or even our English downs awaken," but would "often glance towards the distant and frequently-receding line of the horizon, and wish it gained and passed"; and the "gloomy silent commonwealth" in which the Shakers isolate themselves. The few agreeable places such as Cincinnati, "cheerful, thriving, and animated," or West Point, with its "beauty and freshness," are too briefly dealt with to counteract the overwhelming impression of imprisonment.

Dickens' gloomy verdict on America in his *Notes* can be attributed partly to his mauling at the hands of the American press, partly to what we now call culture shock, which did not hit him until New York, and partly, I think, to certain qualities within him such as impatience and a passion for tidiness and order. Whatever else America was, it was not tidy and, outside such long-settled communities as Boston, it was still very much in the process of becoming organised. Harry Stone writes:

> [Dickens] was unable to see America with the eyes of the immigrant, the settler, the visionary . . . [he] had no realistic conception of America as a growing, expanding nation . . . He despised the rickety settlements along the Ohio because they

*West Point and
the highlands*

were rickety settlements and aspired to be more. There was no
belief in what they might become; there was no understanding
of what the people who lived in those settlements were
doing . . . To Dickens the log cabin was a crude hut, not a
transitory item of pioneer society . . . earth was a mixture of
decay and corruption, not rich organic matter, fertile and
yet to be plundered.[44]

It is possible that if he had actually gone to Australia, as he later contemplated doing, he would have had the same reaction there. Never
having seen it, however, he could continue to imagine it as a thriving,
briskly developing country, where the Micawbers, the Peggottys, Mr.
Mell, the poor schoolmaster, and even that dejected magdalen, Martha,
could all begin a new life and contribute to the building up of a new
society. He sent not only fictional characters there but also two of his

44. Harry Stone, "Dickens' Use of his American Experiences in *Martin
Chuzzlewit*," *PMLA*, vol. 72 (1957), pp. 464–478.

own sons. The only member of the Dickens family to emigrate to America, on the other hand, was the novelist's scapegrace youngest brother, Augustus, who deserted his English wife and children, made a bigamous marriage in Chicago, and died in 1866, having come to little good.

But it cannot just have been Dickens' inability to enter into the feelings of a new citizen of a developing country that made him so unfavourable to America. The brief description of his visit to Canada in chapter 15 of the *Notes* is very different in tone from his account of America. "Few Englishmen are prepared to find it what it is," he writes. "Advancing quietly; old differences settling down, and being fast forgotten; public feeling and private enterprise alike in a sound and wholesome state; nothing of flush or fever in its system, but health and vigour throbbing in its steady pulse: it is full of hope and promise." It was not so much a failure of imagination as an overstimulation of it by the unexpectedly alien quality of the land and its people that formed Dickens' 1842 attitude toward America. To bring forth the fruits of his imaginative experience he needed not the constricting form of a travel book but the liberation of fiction.

III

The readers of *Martin Chuzzlewit*, Dickens' first novel to appear after his return home, were warned by the publishers' advertisements not to expect an American story but one of "English life and manners." By the time the fifth monthly number appeared in May 1843, however, Dickens, seeing that sales needed stimulating, decided that he would immediately draw on his American experiences. Accordingly, his young architect-hero suddenly announces to his affrighted confidant, Tom Pinch, that he has formed the "desperate resolution" of seeking work in America. In the next number we discover that he has no intention of remaining there but, rather, expects to quickly amass a heap of dollars and return to England to claim the bride denied him by poverty and the apparent enmity of his rich grandfather.[45]

Dickens scholars have spilled much ink in debating how far Martin's American excursion may be said to damage the novel's structure,

---

45. "My sentiment is," wrote Dickens to the actor Macready on the eve of the latter's departure for a tour in America, "success to the United States as a golden campaigning ground, but blow the United States to 'tarnal smash as an Englishman's place of residence" (Nonesuch *Letters*, vol. 2, p. 117).

but we are not concerned with that question here. Our business is with the American scenes themselves, considered in isolation. These scenes, Dickens' most sustained exercise in satire since the opening chapters of *Oliver Twist*, have generally been found too shrill, sour, and monotonous by readers on both sides of the Atlantic, but I do not share this view myself. I find them extremely funny. Harry Stone has objected that the lionisation of the obscure young Martin by the Americans as he travels south to take possession of the land he has bought in the Mississippi settlement of Eden is simply "an absurdity which turns Dickens's indignation into farce and his realism into caricature." But absurd farce and caricature are, of course, the essential *modi operandi* of all great satire, and it is satire that Dickens is writing as he gleefully distils that "essence of comicality" largely excluded from *American Notes*. He is no more attempting a realistic portrayal of America than is Nathanael West in *A Cool Million* (a book which owes almost as much to the American scenes in *Chuzzlewit* as it does to Voltaire's *Candide*). If he had been intending to be fair to America he would have caused his hero to land in his beloved Boston rather than in "that damnable jungle . . . of false pretensions and humbug," New York, where for him the American Dream had begun to turn decidedly sour. As for Martin's lionisation, it is absolutely central to Dickens' attack on the Americans' fatal worship of clever fraud and unscrupulous swindling. James Kincaid has made this point very well:

> The saints of this society [Dickens' America] are its most competent scoundrels. Because of this perverted ethic, it is not only consistent but brilliantly apt that they should lionise Martin after they find he has "purchased a 'location' in the Valley of Eden." Dickens is simply showing their most natural urge: to collect in a pack and howl over the victim of their smartness.[46]

Eden turns out to be nothing more than a fever-ridden swamp, and Martin and his faithful servant, Mark Tapley, escape with their lives (to the great disgust of the Americans) only through a fictive device, Mr. Bevan, the one good American in the novel. I call Mr. Bevan a fictive device because he is, in the terms of this novel, an impossible character, as there can be "no sich a person" as a good American any more than there could be a good Yahoo in Book IV of *Gulliver's Travels*. This is most obvious in his speech, for he speaks good standard English rather than the wonderfully inflated jargon that charac-

---

46. James R. Kincaid, *Dickens and the Rhetoric of Laughter* (London: Oxford University Press, 1971), p. 146.

terises all the other Americans, the meaninglessness of which neatly parallels Mr. Pecksniff's brand of sanctimonious oratory back in England.

Mr. Bevan is a definite embarrassment, because it is basic to Dickens' satire that Americans are all the same – boastful, hypocritical, fraudulent, crude in their manners, rapaciously materialist, and either grossly philistine ("Darn your books!" says one) or intellectually pretentious to a grotesque degree. In this vast land of untrammelled individual freedom for everyone with a white skin we find only interchangeable specimens of the lowest common denominator of humanity:

> . . . wherever half a dozen people were collected together, there, in their looks, dress, morals, manners, habits, intellect and conversation, were Mr. Jefferson Brick, Colonel Diver, Major Pawkins, General Choke and Mr. La Fayette Kettle, over, and over, and over again. They did the same things; said the same things; judged all subjects by, and reduced all subjects to, the same standard.

What is astonishing is the way in which Dickens' "endless fertility of laughter-causing detail"[47] makes this sameness so entertaining. It "surprises us by a fine excess," as Keats said poetry should. Just when we are beginning to think that Dickens must surely have exhausted the comic potentialities of American public rhetoric, he produces the Hon. Elijah Pogram and his superbly fatuous eulogy of Mr. Chollop (see extract 67) and carries us on to the final disintegration of meaning in the impassioned froth of the Transcendental lady in a wig (extract 68).

The Americans in *Chuzzlewit* are, in fact, a great Dickens character in composite form. Like Scrooge or Micawber or Pecksniff they always talk in the same way and do the same kind of thing whenever they appear; our delight in them stems from Dickens' apparently inexhaustible ability to intensify, and elaborate on, an essentially simple caricature. Moreover, the Dickensian American as portrayed in *Chuzzlewit* crops up from time to time in Dickens' later writings, for example, in the short story "To Be Read at Dusk" (1852), where he mentions

> the American gentleman in the travellers' parlour of the [Great St. Bernard] convent, who, sitting with his face to the fire, had undertaken to realise to me the whole progress of events

---

47. Walter Bagehot's phrase. See his essay on Dickens in his *Literary Studies* (Everyman's Library Edition, 1911), vol. 2, p. 180.

which had led to the accumulation by the Honorable Ananias Dodger of one of the largest accumulations of dollars ever made in our country.[48]

And, just as he was always delighted to observe the living originals of his great drolls running true to form – Mrs. Nickleby, sitting bodily before him and asking him if he really believed such a woman could exist, or Alderman Cute absurdly denying the existence of Jacob's Island[49] – so was he charmed to find Americans living up to his *Chuzzlewit* caricature. Mr. Colman's naïve ecstasies over the details of English aristocratic life, for example (see extract 73), might have come straight from the pen of Martin's snobbish New York host, Mr. Norris (extracts 58 and 59), and, at the opera in Rome in 1853, Dickens derived much amusement from watching the antics of some genially Chuzzlewittian Americans:

All the seats are numbered arm-chairs, and you buy your number at the pay-place, and go to it with the easiest direction on the ticket itself. We were early, and the four places of the Americans were on the next row behind us – all together. After looking about them for some time, and seeing the greater part of the seats empty (because the audience generally wait in a caffè which is part of the theatre), one of them said "Waal I dunno – I expect we ain't no call to set so nigh to one another neither – will you scatter Kernel, will you scatter sir?" – Upon this the Kernel "scattered" some twenty benches off; and they distributed themselves (for no earthly reason apparently but to get rid of one another) all over the pit. As soon as the overture began, in came the audience in a mass. Then the people who had got the numbers into which they had "scattered", had to get them out; and as they understood nothing that was said to them, and could make no reply but "A-mericani," you may imagine the number of cocked hats it took to dislodge them. At last they were all got back into their right places, except one. About an hour afterwards when Moses (*Moses in Egypt* was the opera) was invoking the darkness, and there was a dead silence all over the house, unwonted sounds of disturbance broke out from a distant corner of the pit, and here and there a beard

48. Dickens mimics American English in this passage by his use of the verb "to realise." Cf. Nonesuch *Letters*, vol. 2, p. 218, where he writes to Macready, "We don't at all take to the idea of your going away, and can't, as our American friends say, 'realise' it."

49. See Forster, p. 280, and *Oliver Twist*, ed. K. Tillotson (Oxford: Clarendon Edition, 1966), p. lxv.

got up to look. "What is it neow, sir?" said one of the Americans to another; "some person seems to be getting along, again streem." "Waal sir" he replied "I dunno. But I xpect 'tis the Kernel sir, a holdin on." So it was. The Kernel was ignominiously escorted back to his right place, not in the least disconcerted, and in perfectly good spirits and temper.[50]

The only major American character to appear in Dickens' fiction after *Chuzzlewit* is not at all like this, however. Captain Jorgan ("Silas Jonas Jorgan, Salem, Massachusetts, United States") is the hero of the 1860 Christmas story, "A Message from the Sea," written jointly by Dickens and Wilkie Collins. He is a shrewd yet kindly man, closely based on a much admired original, Captain Elisha Ely Morgan, to whom Dickens once wrote, "Every short letter from you comes to me like a wholesome breeze from the other side of the Atlantic, giving me assurance that fine natures and sound hearts will never die out of any land so long as the rainbow shines."[51] R. B. Heilman calls the fictional character "rather a Hollywood synthesis" into which Dickens tried "to put the best virtues of Jonathan and Uncle Sam"[52] but, in fact, Dickens, on first introducing Jorgan, at once undercuts any willingness to ascribe his virtues to his nationality: "He was an American born, was Captain Jorgan – a New Englander – but he was a citizen of the world, and a combination of most of the best qualities of most of its best countries." Like Mr. Bevan in *Chuzzlewit* he speaks in standard British English, except when referring satirically to his fellow Americans ("'One of old Parvis's fam'ly I reckon,' said the captain, 'kept a dry-goods store in New York city, and realised a handsome competency by burning his house to ashes'"),[53] and is, to all intents and purposes, not American at all. As a counterbalance to the *Chuzzlewit* Americans he is about as effective as the saintly old Jew, Riah, in *Our Mutual Friend* is in counterbalancing Fagin. Moreover, Riah is clearly intended as an atonement to the Jewish people for the creation of Fagin, but Captain Jorgan is the product of Dickens' desire to pay a graceful compliment to an admired acquaintance, who happened to be American, rather than of any intention to recompense the American people for the flaying he had given them in *Chuzzlewit* – a flaying that had made them, he happily reported to Forster, "stark staring raving mad."[54]

---

50. Forster, pp. 583–584.
51. Quoted by W. J. Carlton in his "Captain Morgan – *Alias* Jorgan," *The Dickensian*, vol. 53 (1957), pp. 75–82.
52. Heilman, "The New World in Charles Dickens's Writings."
53. Cf. also note 7.   54. Forster, p. 309.

IV

Eugene Didier, reviewing *The Letters of Charles Dickens*[55] in *The North American Review* for March 1880, wrote:

> We regret to say that nothing in his correspondence removes from our mind the impression that Dickens's feeling towards America was something like Dean Swift's feeling for mankind – he hated mankind, but loved a few men – Pope, Gay, Bolingbroke, etc.: so Dickens disliked America but he liked a few Americans – Irving, Longfellow, Fields, and "one Mr. Childs", a newspaper proprietor . . .

Allowing for a modification in favour of Boston, this impression is certainly likely to be the one formed by anyone studying Dickens' correspondence between the publication of *Chuzzlewit* and his second visit to the United States in 1867/68. His letters to his American friends are quite as warm and affectionate as his letters to other friends, and he will even go out of his way to say agreeable things to them about their fellow Americans: he tells George Washington Putnam in 1851, "I see many Americans in London, and find them the old good-humoured kind-hearted people."[56] But in his letters to English friends his allusions to America are usually pretty caustic. Writing to Macready in 1844, he refers to America as "that low, coarse and mean Nation . . . perpetually playing skittles with different sets of Idols." And in the same year he declared to Jane Carlyle, after she had met an apparently very Chuzzlewittian American general: "it is *impossible*, following them in their own direction, to caricature that people. I lay down my pen in despair sometimes when I read what I have done, and find how it halts behind my own recollection."[57] An agreeable sojourn in republican Switzerland moves him to make some comparisons unfavourable to America (the Swiss were often called "the Americans of the Continent" but this, Dickens believed, was "the greatest injustice" to them).[58] "They are a genuine people, these Swiss," he wrote to Forster. "There is better metal in them than in all the stars and stripes of all the fustian banners of the so called and falsely called U-nited States."[59] To his Swiss friend, Emile de la Rue, he writes, "I don't

---

55. Edited by his eldest daughter, "Mamie," and his sister-in-law, Georgina Hogarth.
56. Nonesuch *Letters*, vol. 2, p. 332.
57. *Pilgrim*, vol. 4, pp. 10 and 33.
58. Forster, p. 402.
59. Nonesuch *Letters*, vol. 1, p. 777. "Parisian workpeople and smaller shopkeepers," on the other hand, he found even worse than their American

know the American Gentleman – God forgive me for putting two such words together! – whose name you mention,"[60] and he goes on to joke about the way in which so many Americans pretend to be intimately acquainted with him. To Angela Burdett Coutts he writes in 1850 (about a beneficiary of her charity who received funds administered to him by Dickens): "Mr. Devlin is now going to America and (although I find it difficult to understand how *that* can do anybody good) we have descried hopefulness in giving him the rest [of your bounty]."[61] And to Frederick Lehmann, travelling to America in 1862, he writes, "Heaven speed you in that distracted land of troublesome vagabonds."[62]

References to America and Americans in his miscellaneous writings are not generally very friendly, either. In his burlesque teetotal version of Cinderella (in "Frauds on the Fairies," published in *Household Words* in 1853 as a protest against his former artistic collaborator George Cruikshank's attempts to moralise traditional fairy tales), Cinderella's grandmother instructs her to fetch that "virtuously democratic vegetable," an American pumpkin -- "American because in some parts of that independent country, there are prohibitory laws against the sale of alcoholic drinks in any form. Also: because America produced (among many great pumpkins) the glory of her sex, Mrs. Colonel Bloomer.[63] None but an American pumpkin will do, my child." Later, in an *Uncommercial Traveller* essay, "Poor Mercantile Jack," he describes an American sailor seen in Liverpool: "Loafing Jack of the Stars and Stripes, rather an unpromising customer, with his long nose, lank cheeks, high cheek-bones, and nothing soft about him but his cabbage-leaf hat." Even his pleasant reminiscences about American inns (extract 76) are not quite innocent of mockery, but here at least he does allow that he himself should take some of the blame for his quarrel with America. Publicly, of course, he always

---

counterparts: "To the American indifference and carelessness, they add a procrastination and want of the least heed of keeping a promise or being exact, which is certainly not surpassed in Naples. They have the American semi-sentimental independence too, and none of the American vigour or purpose" (Nonesuch *Letters*, vol. 1, p. 812).

60. *Pilgrim*, vol. 4, p. 265.

61. *The Heart of Charles Dickens as revealed in his Letters to Angela Burdett Coutts*, ed. Edgar Johnson (New York, 1952), p. 177.

62. Nonesuch *Letters*, vol. 3, p. 300.

63. Dickens had happily joined in his countrymen's derision of poor Mrs. Bloomer and her campaign to reform women's clothing along more practical and emancipated lines: see his article, "Sucking Pigs," published in *Household Words*, 8 November 1851, and reprinted in *Miscellaneous Papers*, ed. B. W. Matz (London: Chapman and Hall, 1908).

asserted that he was prejudiced in America's favour rather than otherwise, as in his 1850 preface to the Cheap Edition of *American Notes* (extract 74). To an admirer in Tennessee who wrote him in 1859 to suggest that some sort of retraction or apology to the American people would be much welcomed, he replied,

> I cannot take the course you recommend to me simply because I really have nothing to explain away. What I have written of the more ludicrous and dangerous tendencies that I observed in America, I have written quite honestly, and in no unkinder spirit than I have written of innumerable things at home. I have, as any rational man must have, a great interest in America; and I have many dear friends who are the born and bred children of the United States.

He then quotes from the new preface to *American Notes*, characterising the assertion that he is anti-American as a "very foolish thing," and concludes, "I have no belief whatever in the durability of foolish things among a great and sensible people, and I confidently trust myself in the long run to their good humour and sagacity."[64]
But when, a few years later, the "great and sensible people" found themselves embroiled in a fierce civil war, Dickens could not resist crowing a little. In March 1862 he published in *All The Year Round* a piece entitled "The Young Man from the Country." The article opens,

> A song of the hour, now in course of being sung and whistled in every street, the other day reminded the writer of these words . . . that twenty years ago, a little book on the United States, entitled *American Notes*, was published by "a Young Man from the Country," who had just seen and left it.

---

64. Letter quoted by James D. Rust in his note, "Dickens and the Americans," *Nineteenth Century Fiction*, vol. 11 (1956/57), pp. 70–72. One can only speculate what Dickens' feelings would have been had he seen his letter printed in the *Memphis Morning Bulletin* with the following prefatory remarks (also quoted by Rust): "we cannot but say that we *like* his candor and truthfulness. During his visit to this country, DICKENS had but little opportunity of seeing the real 'people', through the crevices in the crowd of toadies and flunkies who flocked around the celebrity . . . If he will come out here to Memphis, *incog.*, and spend a few months with us in the vigorous atmosphere of the Empire of the Mississippi – shoot and fish with us in the wilds of Arkansas, and catch the spirit of those ministers of 'King Cotton' who here do congregate – renew his youth at one of our Memphis Press Dinners, and so get to know our 'folks' that the children will long to go rollicking with him in Court Square – we guaranty [*sic*] to send him home again with impressions, the free expression of which will flatter quite as much as anything he has ever written heretofore displeased."

This Young Man from the Country fell into a deal of trouble, by reason of having taken the liberty to believe that he perceived in America downward popular tendencies for which his young enthusiasm had been anything but prepared. It was in vain for the Young Man to offer in extenuation of his belief that no stranger could have set foot on those shores with a feeling of livelier interest in the country, and stronger faith in it, than he. Those were the days when the Tories had made their Ashburton Treaty,[65] and when the Whigs and Radicals must have no theory disturbed. All three parties waylaid and mauled the Young Man from the Country, and showed that he knew nothing about the country.

Dickens then proceeds to quote at length his adverse judgment of Congress in *American Notes* and his condemnation of American suspiciousness and worship of "smartness" (extracts 48 and 54) and ends:

The foregoing was written in the year eighteen hundred and forty-two. It rests with the reader to decide whether it has received any confirmation, or assumed any colour of truth in or about the year eighteen hundred and sixty-two.

This article is one of the very few devoted to an American subject that Dickens wrote after *Chuzzlewit*. But it would be a very incomplete account of Dickens' dealings with America that omitted any description of the treatment of American subjects in his weekly journals, *Household Words* and *All The Year Round*. Harry Stone has amply documented the strict editorial control that Dickens exercised over at least the first of these journals, which ran from 1850 to 1859, when, following a quarrel with his publishers, he replaced it with *All The Year Round*: "With the inner circles [of contributors] he rigidly controlled what was written and how it was written; with more independent or casual contributors, he exercised control through rejection or through thorough editing."[66] Public identification of Dickens' own views with those expressed by his contributors was encouraged by the printing of the legend "CONDUCTED BY CHARLES DICKENS" immediately below the magazine's title on the first page of every issue and by the anonymous presentation of all contributions.

About two dozen articles concerned with America appeared during the nine years of *Household Words*' existence, not a very great num-

---

65. This treaty, signed in August 1842, settled the northeast boundary dispute between Canada and America. Lord Ashburton was the British signatory.

66. *The Uncollected Writings of Charles Dickens: Household Words 1850–1859*, edited with an introduction and notes by Harry Stone (London: Allen Lane: Penguin Press, 1969), vol. 1, p. 15.

ber when one considers that each weekly issue contained on the average half a dozen items. There was much public interest in California around 1850 as a result of the '49 gold rush, and we find five articles about life there in the early volumes of the journal, including an account of a lynching and some enthusiastic letters from a female English emigrant. "We have been so happy since we came to this part of the world," she reports, but she also says, "should we make much money we intend going to New Zealand, as we like that, much, for cheap living."[67] There is also a sprinkling of articles, over the years, about frontier life (gambling saloons in Arkansas, fighting the Indians in Tennessee or Minnesota, etc.) and about the establishment of new settlements, for example, "Germans in Texas" (25 April 1857), in which Dickens must have been pleased to recognize the appearance of his *Chuzzlewit* Americans. A young German emigrant delights in his political liberty but deplores the dearth of social amenities:

> These American gentlemen, here in Texas, they do not know any pleasure. When they come together sometimes, what do they do? They can only sit all round the fire and speet! Why, then they drink some whiskey; or may be they play cards, or they make a great row. They have no pleasure as in Germany.

Still more Chuzzlewittian are the Americans observed by Sherman Hill, a cultivated young Bostonian, as he travels from St. Louis to St. Paul across the monotonous horror of the prairie ("a desert with none of the charms of the desert") and by steamboat on the Mississippi, where he is trapped as Dickens was by a terrible Yankee bore who "would buttonhole the nearest man and read him asleep with extracts from his diary." "The Western people," says Hill,

> appear to do nothing for the love of doing it. They do not enjoy life. They have no choice or relish of food apparently, but feed themselves with what is nearest, as if they thought eating a thing to be done, and done quickly.

Having gobbled their meal in ten minutes, they "may be seen picking their teeth with their forks, or squirting tobacco-juice, their appetites fully satisfied." It is not surprising, as Anne Lohrli points out, that Dickens should have been moved to send Hill an enthusiastic letter

---

67. "A Woman's Experiences in California" (1 February 1851) and "A 'Ranch' in California" (9 August 1851). For the authorship of these articles, and all others in *Household Words*, see Anne Lohrli's edition of the Household Words *Contributors' Book* (Toronto: University of Toronto Press, 1973).

about this particular article, which might seem a sort of postscript to *Chuzzlewit*.

The American topic that recurs most frequently in *Household Words* is, of course, slavery. Dickens published several articles, including one by Harriet Martineau, dwelling on the horrors of slavery and the slave trade. To "North American Slavery" (18 September 1852), by one of his staff writers, Henry Morley, he himself added some lavish praise of Harriet Beecher Stowe's "noble work," *Uncle Tom's Cabin*.[68] Conceding that Mrs. Stowe's slaves must be "rare specimens," he yet declares that "the details of the slave system among which they live have been carefully collected, and are represented, bright or black, fairly and with all due variety, so that they may be generally accepted as remarkable pictures of the every day truth." In August 1856 he published "American Party Names" by the distinguished American landscape architect and fervent abolitionist Frederick Law Olmsted, which made it clear to English readers who the "goodies" were in the American presidential election that year:

> The platform of the republican party may be condensed into
> three sentences. First, they want Congress to rule the territories
> and exclude slavery therefrom; second they want the restora-
> tion of the Missouri compromise,[69] third, they want to respect
> the rights of other nations . . . the Democrats want – first, Con-
> gress not to meddle with the territories; second Kansas to be
> a slave state; third, to acquire more territory suitable for the
> further extension of slavery without regard to the rights
> of anyone.

As regards America generally, Dickens allows his old acquaintance, Thomas Grattan, who had been British consul in Boston during his 1842 visit, to mock at the national "levity and conceit" in "American Changes of Names" (22 November 1856) and W. B. Jerrold to satirise American manners in "Manners Made to Order" (2 May 1857), a book of etiquette for American ladies, but such easy jeering at things American is rare in the magazine's pages. Even that "material, emi-

---

68. See Stone's *Uncollected Writings of Charles Dickens*, vol. 2, pp. 433–442. For Dickens' later revulsion of feeling with regard to Mrs. Stowe see Stone's "Charles Dickens and Harriet Beecher Stowe," *Nineteenth Century Fiction*, vol. 12 (1957), pp. 188–202, and H. L. Knight's "Dickens and Mrs. Stowe," *Dickens Studies Annual*, vol. 5 (1976), pp. 43–58.

69. The Missouri Compromise was the name given to the arrangement arrived at by Congress during 1819 to 1821 whereby Missouri was admitted as a state of the Union but restrictions on slavery were imposed. The compromise was done away with in 1854.

*Harriet Beecher
Stowe*

nently Jonathonian form of Christianity," Mormonism, is not denied
some virtues in James Hannay's article "In the Name of the Prophet
– Smith!" (19 July 1851), though Dickens did give the piece its satirical title and cautioned his subeditor, "for God's sake don't leave in
anything about such a man [Smith] believing in himself – which he has
no right to do and which would by inference justify almost anything."[70]

Perhaps the most interesting *Household Words* article on an American subject from our point of view is George Augustus Sala's "Colonel Grunpeck and Mr. Parkinson" (14 April 1855). Sala was one of
Dickens' special protégés, a regular contributor to the journal and one
whose work Dickens very freely edited. And as Sala deliberately imi-

---

70. Nonesuch *Letters*, vol. 2, p. 325.

tated Dickens' style people must in any case have often imagined his work actually to be Dickens'. In this particular piece Sala elaborately depicts an American straight out of *Chuzzlewit*, one Colonel Grunpeck of Kentucky, whose

> hatred and contempt for this country and its inhabitant Britishers were something dreadful. He took the British lion; he twisted that animal's tail, and tied knots in it; he tore out the hair of his mane; he cut off his claws; he skinned him alive; he muzzled him; he made him stand on his hind legs and beg; he whipped him through creation, as one would a puppy-dog . . .

Sala then goes on to wonder

> whether we, on our side of the Atlantic, could show any English Grunpecks, any genuine Britishers, who, having visited the United States, had been unable or unwilling to discern one single thing worthy of admiration in their travelling experiences.

He surveys the multitude of travel books about America written by British tourists but, though he finds in them "the people, the manners, and the institutions of the American republic commented on with sufficient severity," he cannot discover "the real prejudiced traveller – the genuine Britisher – who couldn't or wouldn't find any good in the Americans" until he lights on Richard Parkinson's vitriolic *A Tour in America*, published in 1805, which he proceeds to make sport of for the rest of the article. To American readers this article must surely have seemed almost a calculated insult, especially if they believed it to be by Dickens, as they had some excuse for doing. First the world of Chuzzlewittian America is strongly evoked in Colonel Grunpeck and then, blandly ignoring the controversial productions of Basil Hall, Mrs. Trollope, and Dickens himself, the writer declares that he has to go back to some obscure, forgotten work, published half a century earlier, before he can find an example of a really prejudiced British account of America. Dickens cannot have been unaware of the teasing effect this article was bound to have on American readers, and we must, I think, regard its publication in *Household Words* as deliberately provocative on his part.

The United States received far more attention in *All The Year Round* than in *Household Words*. Upwards of sixty articles on American subjects appeared in the former journal between its inauguration in 1859 and Dickens' death eleven years later. Lacking the sort of evidence about contributors that survives for the earlier periodical, we cannot be quite so sure about the closeness of Dickens' editorial supervision of *All The Year Round*, but his letters would certainly seem to indicate that he continued to exercise, both directly and through his subeditor, W. H. Wills, a tight control over its contents. Certainly, as far as the American Civil War is concerned, it has been convincingly shown, as we shall see, that the marked change in editorial policy toward the end of 1861 was due to Dickens himself.

We find in *All The Year Round* articles on all aspects of American life and manners – public transport, Indians, marriage customs, volunteer firemen, elections, cemeteries, newspaper sensations, naval and military traditions, theatres, social discourse, and humour. The pervading tone is a mixture of shocked disapproval, amused patronage, and some admiration. There is a constant fascination with the "go-ahead" vigour of America but also much nervousness about the wilder and more reckless aspects of this. One writer, describing (20 April 1861) an agricultural exhibition in Virginia which included some bear baiting, observes:

> No nervous man (nervousness is not fear) should go to America;
> for a life is thought nothing of in the country that all Europe
> helps to people. Thousands go to see Blondin break his neck
> at Niagara. . . . When two engines are racing to a fire, the two
> companies will pull out revolvers and fight for precedency.
> Duelling is common. Racing steamers will refuse to stop and pick
> up a black hand that has fallen overboard. As for these railway
> crossings, a car driver has been known to put his horses at
> full speed, and bet five dollars he would get over before "the
> darned engine", at the risk of an immortal and irretrievable
> smash.

This kind of excitement is at its most intense, of course, in the dozen or so articles dealing with frontier life in the Far West, in Texas, or in Arkansas. Dickens' readers are here regaled with anecdotes of lynchings, bowie knives, gouging matches, and vigilantes, all of which must have been highly gratifying to the Victorian appetite for stories of sensational violence, preferably true ones.

The Mormons of Utah offer a different kind of sensation, the scandal of their institutionalized polygamy, and three articles on them appeared over the eleven years.[71] Their social and economic achieve-

---

71. *All The Year Round*, vol. 5 (24 August 1861), pp. 509–511; vol. 10 (7 November 1863), pp. 247–252; vol. 17 (9 March 1867), pp. 252–256. On 4 July 1863 Dickens published, in his *Uncommercial Traveller* series, an article describing a Mormon emigration party getting ready to leave London on board the packet ship *Amazon*. Strongly impressed, despite himself, by the emigrants' orderliness, sterling qualities of character, and excellent appearance, Dickens concluded: "What is in store for the poor people on the shores of

ments could not be denied ("No beggars are seen in these long straight dusty green-lined streets – scarcely even a tipsy man . . . The people are quiet and civil"), but the *All The Year Round* writers are less sympathetic to the "monstrous system" of Mormonism than Hannay was in *Household Words*: "despite all the advances of education and of science, men remain more inclined to follow impulse than reason, and more willing to accept an absurdity offered to them than to think for themselves."

Just as Dickens himself had sported with American English in his *Notes* and *Chuzzlewit*, so his contributors in *All The Year Round* continued to divert their readers with what seemed to them the oddities of American speech, sometimes even commenting on the very same phrases as he himself had done:

> To enjoy yourself is to *"have a good time"*. This phrase, which
> I peculiarly dislike from a kind of silly quaintness there is in it,
> was in every one's mouth [in Boston]. *"To be raised"* is to be
> brought up, or reared. *"To judge"* is to think or to imagine. . . .
> In some of the newspapers the rule of writing appears to be
> never to use a short word when you can find a long one. Thus
> you must not say to give, but to *"donate"*.[72]

For one commentator, writing in October 1863, this is no laughing matter. "Our mother English," he laments, "is threatened with a deluge of barbarisms" stemming chiefly from the United States: "fond as we are of rating our republican kinsmen for their vulgarity and uncouthness, it is wonderful to see the eager quickness with which we adopt their perversions of the language." One of his examples is the use of "expect" to mean "suspect."

By far the most important American subject of the years 1860 to 1864 was, of course, the Civil War but, by comparison with other British journals, *All The Year Round*'s coverage of this ferocious upheaval was somewhat meagre. As we have seen, *Household Words* had featured a few antislavery articles and we find one or two more appearing in *All The Year Round* in 1860 and 1861, but Dickens early

---

the Great Salt Lake, what happy delusions they are labouring under now, on what miserable blindness their eyes may be opened then, I do not pretend to say. But I went on board their ship to bear testimony against them if they deserved it, as I fully believed they would; to my great astonishment they did not deserve it; and my predispositions and tendencies must not affect me as an honest witness." See further Richard J. Dunn's "The Unnoticed Uncommercial Traveller," *The Dickensian*, vol. 64 (1968), pp. 103–104.

72. "Our Cousins' Conversation," *All The Year Round*, vol. 11 (16 April 1864), pp. 224–227.

WHY DON'T YOU TAKE IT?

took the line that slavery had really nothing to do with the causes of
the war, which he expected to be "very short" and soon succeeded by
"some new compact between the Northern and the Southern States."[73]
In May 1861 one of his contributors declared that "trade jealousy"
was at the bottom of the "intense virulence of hatred existing between
the Northerns and the Southerns." As to slavery, it "needs no sword
to kill it. It is fast passing away; and it has been proved unprofit-
able."[74] Two articles later in the year are concerned with the necessity
for Britain to look elsewhere than the American South for its raw
cotton, and the second of these again asserts that the war is one of
"tariffs," slavery being a mere "Northern pretext."[75] Just about this
time Dickens read a book, *The American Union,* by an English apol-
ogist for the South, James Spence. He seems to have been totally convinced by it and, as John Waller has shown, the editorial policy of *All
The Year Round* almost immediately became, if not exactly pro-
southern, certainly very hostile to the Federal cause.[76] Dickens fussed
about getting a favourable review of the book (by Henry Morley)
into the journal as quickly as possible, and it duly appeared on 21
December 1861, entitled "American Disunion." Laudatory as it was,

73. Nonesuch *Letters,* vol. 3, p. 209. Dickens was writing in February 1861.
74. "Northern Dog and Southern Cat," *All The Year Round,* vol. 5 (18
May 1861), pp. 181–185.
75. "Our Old and New Cotton Fields," *All The Year Round,* vol. 6 (2
November 1861), pp. 125–128; "Cotton Fields," *All The Year Round,* vol. 6
(7 December 1861), pp. 256–260.
76. John O. Waller, "Charles Dickens and the American Civil War," *Studies
in Philology,* vol. 57 (1960), pp. 535–548.

Dickens was disappointed with it, and a second article by Morley appeared the following week which pursued the argument that the war was "solely a fiscal quarrel": "Union means so many millions a year lost to the South; secession means the loss of the same millions to the North. The love of money is the root of this as of many, many other evils."[77]

Wholeheartedly believing this, Dickens felt sure the war would end in "an ignoble and contemptible compromise." The New Yorkers, "the greatest and meanest of scoundrels," would refuse to accept conscription, he was convinced. He summed up his views in a letter written to a Swiss friend on 16 March 1862:

> I take the facts of the American quarrel to stand thus. Slavery
> has in reality nothing on earth to do with it, in any kind of
> association with any generous or chivalrous sentiment on the part
> of the North. But the North having gradually got to itself the
> making of the laws and the settlement of the Tariff, and having
> taxed the South most abominably for its own advantage, began
> to see as the country grew, that unless it advocated the laying
> down of a geometrical line beyond which slavery should not
> extend, the South would necessarily recover its old political
> power, and be able to help itself a little in the adjustment of com-
> mercial affairs. Any reasonable creature may know, if willing,
> that the North hates the Negro, and that until it was convenient
> to make a pretence that sympathy with him was the cause of
> the war, it hated the abolitionists and derided them up hill and
> down dale. For the rest there is not a pin to choose between the
> two parties. They will both rant and lie and fight until they
> come to a compromise; and the slave may be thrown into that
> compromise or thrown out of it, just as it happens. As to
> Secession being Rebellion, it is distinctly possible by state papers,
> that Washington considered it no such thing – that Massachu-
> setts, now loudest against it, has itself asserted its right to secede,
> again and again.[78]

Waller compares this passage with Spence's book and shows that all Dickens' arguments are clearly derived from that source. Dickens, we note, declares that "there is not a pin to choose between" the Union and the Confederacy, but it is remarkable that *All The Year Round* contained so much about the bravery of Confederate boy-soldiers or

---

77. [Henry Morley], "The Morill Tariff," *All The Year Round*, vol. 6 (28 December 1861), pp. 328–331.
78. Nonesuch *Letters*, vol. 3, pp. 288–289.

of southern belles in beleaguered Mobile, about the daring and gallant exploits of southern blockade runners or the brutal behaviour of the Federal army. The celebrated British actress Fanny Kemble (who had experienced firsthand the wretchedness of being a slave owner's wife on a southern plantation) was apparently moved to reproach him with being a southern sympathiser. He replied,

> I am a Southern sympathiser to this extent – that I no more believe in the Northern love of the black man, or in the North-ern horror of slavery having anything to do with the beginning of the war, save as pretence – than I believe that the Davenport Brothers and their properties are under the special patronage of several angels of distinction.[79]

Certainly, no one looking back at Dickens' comments in *American Notes* on such of the South as he saw could regard him as sympatheti-cally or romantically disposed toward that part of the world. It was rather the case, I think, that he was happy to use the southern cause as a stick with which to belabour his old Yankee enemies, and he cyni-cally regarded the whole war as entirely a matter of dollars and polit-ical power struggles – just such a civil war, in fact, as the corrupt America of *Martin Chuzzlewit* would inevitably embroil itself in.

V

In 1858 Dickens launched himself upon what was, in effect, a whole new career, that of giving paid public readings from his own works. His anticipation that *"a very large sum of money"* would be realised by a series of such readings in London and the provinces during the summer and autumn was triumphantly justified. It was inevitable that he should sooner or later take these readings to that "golden cam-paigning grounds," the United States – where, he wrote in March 1858, "I believe I could make (if I could resolve to go there) ten thousand pounds."[80]

"If I could resolve to go there." Dickens was not at all wanting to return to America for its own sake and was, moreover, rather appre-

---

79. Nonesuch *Letters*, vol. 3, p. 416. The American mediums, Ira Erastus Davenport (1839–1911) and his brother, William H. H. Davenport (1841–1877), toured the United States and Europe between 1860 and 1877 with a highly successful spiritualist act.

80. Nonesuch *Letters*, vol. 3, p. 12. For Dickens' characterisation of America as a "golden campaigning ground" see note 45.

hensive of the sort of reception he might get if he did go there. Some time in the early 1860s he wrote to Captain Morgan,

> Read in America? Humph! Well – if you had fifty thousand children there I would come directly; but you haven't, you see. And my mind strongly misgives me that I should see many faces turned toward me less beaming and kindly than yours. So I won't come just at present.[81]

But the Americans would not let him rest on the subject:

> Every mail brings me proposals . . . A certain Mr. Grau, who took Ristori out, and is highly responsible, wrote to me by the last mail (for the second time) saying that if I would give him a word of encouragement he would come over immediately and arrange on the boldest terms for any number I chose, and would deposit a large sum of money at Coutts's. Mr. Fields writes to me on behalf of a committee of private gentlemen at Boston who wished for the credit of getting me out, who desired to hear the readings and did not want profit, and would put down as a guarantee £10,000 – also to be banked here. Every American speculator who comes to London repairs straight to Dolby [Dickens' readings manager] with similar proposals.[82]

Gradually, Dickens' apprehensions were smoothed away, and as his living expenses rose (with so many relatives of all kinds dependent on him) he became more and more mesmerised by the vision of the heaps of American gold that could be his. "I should be wretched beyond expression there," he wrote to Forster, but in the same month (May 1867) he was telling his housekeeper/sister-in-law that "expenses are so enormous that I begin to feel myself drawn towards America, as Darnay in the Tale of Two Cities was attracted to the Loadstone Rock, Paris."[83] An ominous comparison, and one which Dickens' biographers have not failed to make the most of.[84] "America may well be the death of me" is what he is saying and, indeed, there is no doubt at all that the fearful strain his transatlantic readings tour imposed on

---

81. Quoted by W. J. Carlton in "Captain Morgan – *Alias* Jorgan."

82. Forster, p. 708. Ristori was the internationally acclaimed Italian actress, Adelaide Ristori, who made her triumphant début in America in 1866.

83. Forster, p. 708; Nonesuch *Letters*, vol. 3, p. 527.

84. See, for example, Johnson on Dickens' state after his punishing American tour: "Though in some miraculous way the vessel had not been dashed to pieces against the Loadstone Rock and sunk, all its fabric was twisted and broken with the dreadful strain. Could it attempt another such voyage and not go down? . . ." (*Charles Dickens*, vol. 2, p. 1094).

"Dickens's Farewell to Hamerica." From an unidentified American newspaper, 1868. The verses printed with this cartoon are given in W. Glyde Wilkins' Dickens in Cartoon and Caricature *(ed. B. W. Matz for the Boston Biblio- phile Society, 1924). The following lines are representative:*

Farewell Columbia! Land of soft delight;
Your shores will soon be lost unto my sight
But I will carry to my latest day
The sweet assurance of how well you pay.

. . . .

I hail you from the bottom of my purse
And beg your pardon for my former curse.

his already damaged health did much to hasten his early death.[85]

Two things drove him on. One was that "wind that bloweth all the world beside, desire of gold." He calculated that he would clear a profit of £15,500 on a series of eighty readings and, in the event, cleared £19,000 on seventy-six.[86] He must have derived an intense secret delight from at last making America pay for what he gave it, because his bitterness about the pirating of his books was, if anything, stronger in 1867 than it had been in 1842: "In America the occupation of my life for thirty years is, unless it bears your imprint, utterly worthless and profitless to me," he wrote to the publishers Ticknor and Fields.[87] The second motivating force was the anticipation of a reception by his American audiences so rapturous that it would make even the tremendous demonstrations of affection and delight he had experienced at home seem quite mild. "I am really endeavoring tooth and nail to make my way personally to the American public," he told Fields.[88] Just as he had a quarter century before, he began to savour in advance the delights of a triumphant reception – only, this time, he and not his hosts would be in control. If America wanted him again as a "raree show" it could have him, but on his terms and at his price: "If he went at all, he would go on his own account, making no compact with any one."[89]

His manager, George Dolby, went out to prospect the situation in August 1867. "The Americans are a people whom a fancy does not hold long," Dickens told Forster, and their passion to hear him read

---

85. Dickens convinced himself, however, that there would be less risk to his health on the projected American reading tour than there had been on his first visit: "When I went to America in '42, I was so much younger, but (I think) very much weaker, too. I had had a painful surgical operation performed, shortly before going out, and had had the labour from week to week of Master Humphrey's Clock. My life in the States was a life of continual speech-making (quite as laborious as Reading), and I was less patient and more irritable then, than I am now" (Nonesuch *Letters*, vol. 3, p. 530).

86. Dolby tells us: "Supposing gold to have been at par, it will be seen from the figures named that the profits of the enterprise would have been nearly £38,000; but as Mr. Dickens had no faith in American securities at that time, he preferred to convert the currency we received into gold, paying the difference 39½ per cent., and an additional ¼ per cent. for banker's commission" (*Charles Dickens as I knew him* [1885], p. 332).

87. Nonesuch *Letters*, vol. 3, p. 523. For the furor caused by this too sweeping statement after it had been publicised in the press, see a forthcoming article, "Dickens' Second American Tour and his 'Utterly Worthless and Profitless' American 'Rights,'" by Andrew J. Kappel and Robert L. Patten, scheduled for publication in *Dickens Studies Annual*, vol. 7 (1979).

88. Nonesuch *Letters*, vol. 3, p. 530.

89. Forster, p. 708.

would probably yield to other, political, passions in 1868, a presidential election year, so it was essential to undertake the tour no later than the winter of 1867/68. He no longer, apparently, had any fears about the state of public feeling toward him in America. *American Notes* and *Chuzzlewit* "had no more to do with Mr. Dickens's calculations than if they had never been written," Dolby tells us[90] and, once Dickens had received from his manager a satisfactory report on the halls available and other arrangements, he bore down his best friend's strenuous opposition to the project[91] and determined to go.

He derived some scornful amusement from Dolby's report that the editor of the *New York Herald* believed that if "Dickens would *first*

Dickens "not at home" to his former American acquaintances, Harper's Weekly, *21 December 1867*

90. Dolby, *Charles Dickens*, p. 93.

91. Forster was anxious about Dickens' health but also "had a personal dislike to America and the Americans," according to Dolby: "He was certain there was no money in America, and, even if there were, Mr. Dickens would not get any of it; and if he *did*, the Irish (by some means I could not quite understand), and the booksellers between them, would break into the hotel and rob him of it. Even if the money were deposited in a bank, the bank would fail on purpose" (*Charles Dickens*, p. 137).

'IMPROVED" READINGS IN AMERICA.

RUDOLPH (DOLBY), his agent, commands, in advance, the American public to do reverence to Geisler's [Boz's] hat, previous to its being passed around to collect their cash The Flunkeys obey. William Tell — Bennett — and others resist.

apologise to the American public for the 'Notes' and 'Martin Chuzzlewit' he would make a large amount of money."[92] Dickens was the last man to eat humble pie in this fashion, but he realised that he would have to make some sort of public statement about his relations with, and attitude toward, America before embarking on his tour. Already the New York newspapers were at their old tricks of misrepresenta-

92. Dolby, *Charles Dickens*, p. 124.

Dinner given to Mr Charles Dickens
on the occasion of
His Departure for the United States,
Freemason's Hall, Great Queen St.
Saturday, November 2nd 1867, Seven o'Clock.

Tickets
One Guinea.   28   *Hon. Sec.*

tion and slander. A report of an interview with Dickens appeared in the *Tribune* which was, he telegraphed to Fields, "totally false." It was, Dickens wrote in a follow-up letter, "so absurdly unlike me that I cannot suppose it to be even invented by anyone who ever heard me exchange a word with mortal creature." He was represented as saying, among other things, that he "could not be expected to have an interest in the American people." This he elaborately refuted in his letter to Fields,[93] but some public reassurance was also necessary. An ideal opportunity was provided by the grand farewell banquet offered to him by his friends and admirers in London on 2 November 1867, which would, of course, be very extensively reported in America before his own arrival there. In his speech[94] Dickens observed that "a vast entirely new generation" had arisen in America since his previous visit, that the "best known" of his own books had been published since then (rather hard on *Pickwick Papers* and its three immediate successors, this!), and that the coming together of the new generation and the books had resulted in his receiving "an immense accumulation of letters" inviting him to revisit America, "all expressing in the same hearty, homely, cordial, unaffected way, a kind of personal interest in me." His longing to meet this "multitude of new friends" was taking him across the Atlantic a second time, strengthened by "a natural de-

93. Nonesuch *Letters*, vol. 3, p. 556.
94. See *Speeches of Charles Dickens*, ed. Fielding, pp. 368–374.

"Au Revoir!" Cartoon published in the London comic weekly Judy, *30 October 1867, and reproduced in* Harper's Weekly, *14 December 1867. In* Judy *the cartoon was accompanied by some verses:*

'Twas not without a touch of pride We sent, to greet our Yankee brother, The man whose lessons far and wide Instruct all men to love each other.

sire to see for myself the astonishing change and progress of a quarter of a century over there." (This last reason we may take with a pinch of salt, I think, but it was excellent for public consumption.) Dickens ended by neatly quoting the sentence about motes and beams from his 1855 Christmas story (see extract 76), in which he characterised the Americans as "a kind, generous, large-hearted, and great people," adding, "In that faith I am going to see them again." He was then able to sit down confident that he had amply atoned for *Chuzzlewit* without any such abject grovelling as the *New York Herald* recommended.[95]

In the event, the American readings tour (2 December 1867 to 20 April 1868) was a huge success, marred only by Dickens' persistent ill health and by recurrent troubles with the "noble army of speculators" who, despite all Dolby's vigilance, everywhere bought up tickets for resale at inflated prices. He might have said, with Mercutio, "I have caught an everlasting cold," for the severe catarrh and racking

95. Though, as Fielding notes, "the occasion left some Americans unmollified." He quotes one New Jersey journal as condemning the whole affair as a "Sardanapulian scene," a drunken "orgie" (*Speeches of Charles Dickens*, p. 374).

cough that seized him soon after his arrival in Boston never left him throughout the whole five-month trip; it was impervious even to the "Rocky Mountain Sneezer," a supposedly infallible cure compounded of brandy, rum, and snow pressed on Dickens by his New York land-lord. He endured agonies of sleeplessness and was eventually reduced to a diet consisting entirely of stimulants (rum, sherry, champagne, beef tea) and soup: "I do not eat more than half a pound of solid food in the whole four-and-twenty hours, if so much."[96] The winter was, Forster records, exceptionally severe, "even for America," and the railroad travelling was hard. "It is a bad country to be unwell and travelling in," Dickens wrote his daughter, Mary: "You are one of, say, a hundred people in a heated car with a great stove in it, all the little windows being closed; and the bumping and banging about are indescribable, the atmosphere detestable, and ordinary motion all but intolerable."[97] During the last months of Dickens' visit such physical miseries were greatly intensified by the recurrence of a very pain-ful foot affliction which had last attacked him the previous summer (". . . on the sofa all last night in tortures").[98]

It was a nightly miracle that, under circumstances like these, the "British Lion" was able to roar so superbly whenever he found him-self behind the familiar velvet-covered reading desk and illuminated by those "garish lights." The stupendous enthusiasm of his audiences was a potent drug that banished even "the true American" (Dickens' name

The Russia, *the ship which brought Dickens to America in 1867*

96. Forster, p. 792.   97. Forster, p. 775.   98. Forster, p. 709.

Certificate from Fordyce Barker, M.D.

A Currier and Ives print entitled "Five Minutes for Refreshment"

Cartoon, probably by Thomas Nast, published in a New York newspaper, The Daily Joker, *in 1868*

MR. CHARLES DICKENS'S READING.

I certify that Mr. Dickens is suffering from a Neuralgic Affection of the right foot, probably occasioned by great fatigue in a severe winter. But I believe that he can read to-night without much pain or inconvenience, (his mind being set on not disappointing his audience,) with the aid of a slight mechanical addition to his usual arrangements.

FORDYCE BARKER, M. D.

THE BRITISH LION IN AMERICA (Charles Dickens).—

CHARLES DICKENS.

Entered according to Act of Congress, in the year 1867, by J. GURNEY & SON, in the Clerk's Office of the District Court of the United States, for the Southern District of New York.

J. Gurney & Son   707. Broadway. N.Y.

for his catarrh) so long as he was on stage. Few, seeing him like that, could credit Dolby's accounts of his "Chief's" frequent near-prostration offstage. Fortunately, Dickens was cared for not only by Dolby, whom he described as being "as tender as a woman and as watchful as a doctor," but also by his adoring Boston friends, the publisher James Fields and his wife, Kate. Their home afforded Dickens a highly congenial place of retreat, rest, and recuperation.

He had planned an itinerary which would take in Cincinnati, Pittsburgh, St. Louis, and Chicago but gave up these cities when it became obvious that the tour was proving hugely profitable without them. Moreover, the additional strain on Dickens' health of such enormous journeys could well have been disastrous. "Good heavens, sir," A Philadelphia gentleman remonstrated with him, "if you don't read in Chicago the people will go into fits!" Dickens mildly replied that he would prefer that the Chicagoans should go into fits rather than that he himself should, but the Philadelphian "didn't seem to see it at all."[99] On the other hand, Dickens rejected the suggestion that he should read every week in New York. In order to whip up enthusiasm for his planned farewell readings in that city and in Boston it would be necessary, he thought, having regard to the American character, to put the readings out of the New Yorkers' and Bostonians' reach for a time:

> It is one of the popular peculiarities which I most particularly
> notice, that they must not have a thing too easily. Nothing in this
> country lasts long; and a thing is prized the more, the less easy
> it is made . . . the best thing I can do is not to give either city
> as much reading as it wants now, but to be independent of both
> while both are most enthusiastic.[100]

The first six weeks of the tour were, in fact, devoted entirely to Boston and New York, with Boston, of course, being the first city of all to hear the readings. "Mr. Dickens," Dolby tells us, "always regarded Boston as his American home, inasmuch as all his literary friends lived there, and he felt it to be only due to them that he should make that his starting-place. . . ."[101] Weeks seven and eight were devoted to Philadelphia and Brooklyn (where, to his great amusement, he found himself reading in a church, "appearing out of the vestry in canonical form")[102] and weeks nine, ten, and eleven to Baltimore, Washington,

Dickens, photographed by J. Gurney in New York

---

99. Forster, pp. 781–782.   100. Forster, pp. 772–773.
101. Dolby, *Charles Dickens*, p. 160.
102. Nonesuch *Letters*, vol. 3, p. 598. The minister of the Brooklyn church was the brother of Harriet Beecher Stowe, Henry Ward Beecher.

"Selling Tickets for the Dickens Readings at New York"

and Philadelphia again. Then followed an excursion into New England, a return to Boston, where he also took a week's breather, a hard journey to various towns in upstate New York, New England again, then Portland, Maine, and so back to Boston and, finally, New York.

Dickens was prudently anxious not to give the Americans any new cause for offence. He had instructed his subeditor, Wills, that no reference, however slight, was to be made to America in any article whatever appearing in *All The Year Round* during his tour, and the following anecdote, related in one of his letters home, suggests that the members of his team were under instructions to be careful what they said about America: his dresser, Scott, grumbling about having been turned away from a theatre, said, "it's a beastly country!" whereupon "Majesty" interposed, "Scott, don't you express your opinions about the country," and the irate dresser subsided apologetically (though still murmuring about "beasts in railway cars [spitting] tobacco over your boots").[103] Certainly, Dickens had no intention of gnawing again at that old bone of contention, international copyright,

103. Nonesuch *Letters*, vol. 3, p. 607.

and declined an invitation to address a Boston meeting on the subject.

But the smoother relations between Dickens and his American public on this trip were not simply the result of commercial prudence on the novelist's part. He does genuinely seem, as is apparent from the last few extracts in this anthology, to have felt that vast improvements, social as well as technological, had taken place.[104] When he was questioned about America at a dinner party at the Fields' he was heard to say "that it was very much grown up, indeed he should not know oftentimes that he was not in England, things went on so much the same and with very few exceptions (hardly worth mentioning) he was let alone precisely as he would have been there."[105] The assumption behind this – that America demonstrated its maturity as a nation by becoming ever more like England – might have been acceptable to his Boston friends, but it was as well, perhaps, that Dickens did not pursue this particular line in his farewell speech in New York.

Outside Boston, the differentness of America asserted itself again as it had in 1842. The greater riskiness of daily life, for example: his hotel in New York caught fire but "fires in this country are quite a matter of course," he told his sister-in-law. Along with this higher degree of risk went a tremendous national resilience: Portland had been burnt to the ground three years previously "yet such is the astonishing energy of the people that the large hall in which I am to read tonight (its predecessor was burnt) would compare very favourably with the Free Trade Hall at Manchester."[106]

Chuzzlewittian America had not utterly vanished, of course, and his dresser's saliva-bespattered boots were not the only signs of this. In Baltimore Dickens noticed the cynical political manipulation of the newly enfranchised blacks (see extract 84), and the corruption in the Irish-American-dominated local government in New York was, he believed, "stupendous." The newspapers still reflected the national vanity in a "wonderfully quizzical" fashion: "They seem to take it ill

---

104. His initial impressions, on landing again in Boston, were the opposite. Dolby records: "He had been annoyed at supper by the waiters leaving the door of the sitting-room partially open, that the promenaders in the corridor of the hotel might take a peep at him, through the crack between the door and the doorpost, whilst he was sitting at table. This curiosity made an unpleasant impression in his mind, and caused him to regret that he had not adhered to his original determination never to visit America again; for, he said; 'These people have not in the least changed during the last five and twenty years – they are doing now exactly what they were doing then'" (*Charles Dickens*, pp. 158–159).

105. M. A. DeWolfe Howe, *Memories of a Hostess: A Chronicle of Eminent Friendships drawn chiefly from the Diaries of Mrs. James T. Fields* (Boston, 1922), p. 164.

106. Forster, pp. 772 and 793.

CURIOUS EXPERIENCE OF MR. DICKENS AT DELMONICO'S APRIL 18 1868
HE LISTENS TO A DISCOURSE FROM HIS OWN MR. PICKWICK OR FROM SOMEBODY VERY MUCH
LIKE HIM

Cartoon from an unidentified American newspaper, 1868, included in W. Glyde Wilkins' Dickens in Cartoon and Caricature. The cartoonist is making play with the resemblance to Mr. Pickwick of Horace Greeley, editor of the New York Tribune, who chaired the farewell banquet to Dickens at Delmonico's, 18 April 1868

MR. C—S D—S AND THE HONEST LITTLE BOY
H. L. B. — "HOLLO MISTER, LOOKA HERE YOU'VE DROPPED SUTHIN"

Cartoon by Thomas Nast published in the New York Evening Telegram, April 1868. American cartoonists delighted in attributing a Cockney pronunciation to Dickens, representing him as saying "Hamerica," for example

DOLBY.—" *Well, Mr. Dickens, on the eve of our departure, I present you with $300,000, the result of your Lectures in America.*"
DICKENS.—" *What! only $300,000? Is that all I have made out of these penurious Yankees, after all my abuse of them? Pshaw! Let us go, Dolby!*"

that I don't stagger on to the platform overpowered by the spectacle before me, and the national greatness" (extract 82). But, overall, he had no doubt that there had been "*great changes*" for the better, and he was happy to bear testimony to these in his speech at the New York farewell banquet in his honour. This turned into a veritable love feast after Dickens had pronounced his eloquent tribute to America; and one of the speakers, a Cincinnati journalist, replying to the toast of "the Western Press," even quoted goodhumouredly from the American scenes in *Chuzzlewit* and praised *American Notes* as "an exceedingly clever, good-natured and true book."[107] Not all the American press was ready to forgive Dickens, however, as can be seen from the

107. See W. Glyde Wilkins, *Charles Dickens in America* (London: Chapman and Hall, 1911), p. 289. The speaker, alluding to Elijah Pogram's praise of Chollop, had said, "My home is not 'in the bright setting sun'."

very hostile cartoons reproduced in this volume; in these Dickens is depicted as grabbing as many dollars as he can whilst remaining utterly contemptuous of his hosts. And to this day it is part of the "Dickens legend" that he hated America. His much modified opinions of 1868 are forgotten and only his 1842 opinions remembered.

The truth is, I think, that Dickens was a *natural* American and therefore had just the same love/hate relationship with America as he had with the country of his birth. In his touchy pride, his ruthless energy, his unwavering belief in the rewards of industry, his rejection of the past, and his faith in the future Dickens was very much an American. Had he not been so American in his idealism in 1842, moreover, he would never have been so bitterly bewildered and disappointed by the imperfections he found obtruding themselves on him as he travelled around the country. With a much deeper truth than the late President Kennedy claiming to be a Berliner, Dickens might have said, "I am an American." This anthology documents his lifelong fascination with the country and could well have carried the subtitle "Notes of a Nonnative Son."

I. First impressions: letters from America, 1842

1. Meeting the press

The SS Britannia *arrived in Boston on 22 January. Seven days later Dickens wrote this description of a striking feature of the arrival scene in a letter to Forster.*

As the Cunard boats have a wharf of their own at the custom-house, and that a narrow one, we were a long time (an hour at least) working in. I was standing in full fig on the paddle-box beside the captain, staring about me, when suddenly, long before we were moored to the wharf, a dozen men came leaping on board at the peril of their lives, with great bundles of newspapers under their arms; worsted comforters (very much the worse for wear) round their necks; and so forth. "Aha!" says I, "this is like our London-bridge": believing of course that these visitors were news-boys. But what do you think of their being EDITORS? And what do you think of their tearing violently up to me and beginning to shake hands like madmen? Oh! If you could have seen how I wrung their wrists! And if you could but know how I hated one man in very dirty gaiters, and with very protruding upper teeth, who said to all comers after him, "So you've been introduced to our friend Dickens – eh?"

Customhouse and dock, Boston, where Dickens landed in 1842. From W. Glyde Wilkins' Charles Dickens in America *(London: Chapman and Hall, Ltd., 1911)*

2. Utopia – apparently

To Forster from Boston. The "blind school" was the Perkins Institution discussed at length in American Notes, *chapter 3.*

The American poor, the American factories, the institutions of all kinds – I have a book, already. There is no man in this town, or in this State of New England, who has not a blazing fire and a meat dinner every day of his life. A flaming sword in the air would not attract so much attention as a beggar in the streets. There are no charity uniforms, no wearisome repetition of the same dull ugly dress, in that blind school. All are attired after their own tastes, and every boy and girl has his or her individuality as distinct and unimpaired as you would find it in their own homes. At the theatres, all the ladies sit in the fronts of the boxes. The gallery are as quiet as the dress circle at dear Drury-lane. A man with seven heads would be no sight at all, compared with one who couldn't read and write.

State Street, Boston

The Perkins Institution for the blind, Boston

3. National vanity

To Forster from New York, 17 February. Taglioni was a celebrated ballet dancer of the 1830s.

Now, the phase of character in the Americans which amuses me most, was put before me in its most amusing shape by the circumstances attending this affair. I had noticed it before, and have since, but I cannot better illustrate it than by reference to this theme. Of course I can do nothing but in some shape or other it gets into the newspapers. All manner of lies get there, and occasionally a truth so twisted and distorted that it has as much resemblance to the real fact as Quilp's leg to Taglioni's. But with this ball to come off, the newspapers were if possible unusually loquacious; and in their accounts of me, and my seeings, sayings, and doings on the Saturday night and Sunday before, they describe my manner, mode of speaking, dressing, and so forth. In doing this, they report that I am a very charming fellow (of course), and have a very free and easy way with me; "which," say they, "at first amused a few fashionables;" but soon pleased them exceedingly.

Another paper, coming after the ball, dwells upon its splendour and brilliancy; hugs itself and its readers upon all that Dickens saw; and winds up by gravely expressing its conviction, that Dickens was never in such society in England as he has seen in New York, and that its high and striking tone cannot fail to make an indelible impression on his mind! For the same reason I am always represented, whenever I appear in public, as being "very pale!;" "apparently thunderstruck;" and utterly confounded by all I see. . . . You recognize the queer vanity which is at the root of all this?

4. Home truths

To Forster from New York, 24 February. Scott was Dickens' great example (himself apart) of a British writer who had suffered enormous financial loss due to the absence of any international copyright law.

I believe there is no country, on the face of the earth, where there is less freedom of opinion on any subject in reference to which there is a broad difference of opinion, than in this – There! – I write the words with reluctance, disappointment, and sorrow; but I believe it from the bottom of my soul. I spoke, as you know, of international copyright, at Boston; and I spoke of it again at Hartford. My friends were paralysed with wonder at such audacious daring. The notion that I, a man alone by himself, in America, should venture to suggest to the Americans that there was one point on which they were neither just to their own countrymen nor to us, actually struck the boldest dumb! Washington Irving, Prescott, Hoffman, Bryant, Halleck, Dana, Washington Allston – every man who writes in this country is devoted to the question, and not one of them *dares* to raise his voice and complain of the atrocious state of the law. It is nothing that of all men living I am the greatest loser by it. It is nothing that I have a claim to speak and be heard. The wonder is that a breathing man can be found with temerity enough to suggest to the Americans the possibility of their having done wrong. I wish you could have seen the faces that I saw, down both sides of the table at Hartford, when I began to talk about Scott. I wish you could have heard how I gave it out. My blood so boiled as I thought of the monstrous injustice that I felt as if I were twelve feet high when I thrust it down their throats.

I had no sooner made that second speech than such an outcry began (for the purpose of deterring me from doing the like in this city) as an Englishman can form no notion of. Anonymous letters; verbal dissuasions; newspaper attacks making Colt (a murderer who is attracting great attention here) an angel by comparison with me; assertions that I was no gentleman, but a mere mercenary scoundrel; coupled with the most monstrous mis-representations relative to my design and purpose in visiting the United States; came pouring in upon me every day. The dinner committee here (composed of the first gentlemen in America, remember that) were so dismayed, that they besought me not to pursue the subject *although they every one agreed with me*.

Maiden Lane and Broadway, by J. J. Fogarty

5. Complaints of a Lion

Continuation of the letter to Forster of 24 February.

I have come at last, and it is time I did, to my life here, and intentions for the future. I can do nothing that I want to do, go nowhere where I want to go, and see nothing that I want to see. If I turn into the street, I am followed by a multitude. If I stay at home, the house becomes, with callers, like a fair. If I visit a public institution, with only one friend, the directors come down incontinently, waylay me in the yard, and address me in a long speech. I go to a party in the evening, and am so inclosed and hemmed about by people, stand where I will, that I am exhausted for want of air. I dine out, and have to talk about everything, to everybody. I go to church for quiet, and there is a violent rush to the neighbourhood of the pew I sit in, and the clergyman preaches *at* me. I take my seat in a railroad car, and the very conductor won't leave me alone. I get out at a station, and can't drink a glass of water, without having a hundred people looking down my throat when I open my mouth to swallow. Conceive what all this is! Then by every post, letters on letters arrive, all about nothing, and all demanding an immediate answer. This man is offended because I won't live in his house; and that man is thoroughly disgusted because I won't go out more than four times in one evening. I have no rest or peace, and am in a perpetual worry.

6. American ladies. Liberty endangered

Continuation of the letter to Forster of 24 February.

The ladies of America are decidedly and unquestionably beautiful. Their complexions are not so good as those of Englishwomen; their beauty does not last so long; and their figures are very inferior. But they are most beautiful. I still reserve my opinion of the national character – just whispering that I tremble for a radical coming here, unless he is a radical on principle, by reason and reflection, and from the sense of right. I fear that if he were anything else, he would return home a tory . . . . . I say no more on that head for two months from this time, save that I do fear that the heaviest blow ever dealt at lib-

"The Land of Liberty"

erty will be dealt by this country, in the failure of its example to the earth. The scenes that are passing in Congress now, all tending to the separation of the States, fill one with such a deep disgust that I dislike the very name of Washington (meaning the place, not the man), and am repelled by the mere thought of approaching it.

---

7. American railroads

To Forster from Philadelphia, 6 March.

I have often asked Americans in London which were the better railroads – ours or theirs? They have taken time for reflection, and generally replied on mature consideration that they rather thought we excelled; in respect of the punctuality with which we arrived at our stations, and the smoothness of our travelling. I wish you could see what an American railroad is, in some parts where I now have seen them. I won't say I wish you could feel what it is, because that would be an unchristian and savage aspiration. It is never inclosed, or warded off. You walk down the main street of a large town: and, slap-dash, headlong, pell-mell, down the middle of the street; with pigs burrowing, and boys flying kites and playing marbles, and men smoking, and women talking, and children crawling, close to the very rails; there comes tearing along a mad locomotive with its train of cars, scattering a red-hot shower of sparks (from its *wood* fire) in all directions; screeching, hissing, yelling, and panting; and nobody one atom more concerned than if it were a hundred miles away. You cross a turnpike-

THE BOWERY LOCOMOTIVE, OR THE PLEASURES OF A RAIL-ROAD.

This cartoon followed the introduction of the locomotive into New York City

Interior of a passenger car of the best quality in 1852

road; and there is no gate, no policeman, no signal – nothing to keep the wayfarer or quiet traveller out of the way, but a wooden arch on which is written in great letters "Look out for the locomotive." And if any man, woman, or child, don't look out, why it's his or her fault, and there's an end of it.

The cars are like very shabby omnibuses – only larger; holding sixty or seventy people. The seats, instead of being placed long ways, are put cross-wise, back to front. Each holds two. There is a long row of these on each side of the caravan, and a narrow passage up the centre. The windows are usually all closed, and there is very often, in addition, a hot, close, most intolerable charcoal stove in a red-hot glow. The heat and closeness are quite insupportable. But this is the characteristic of all American houses, of all the public institutions, chapels, theatres, and prisons. From the constant use of the hard anthracite coal in these beastly furnaces, a perfectly new class of diseases is springing up in the country. Their effect upon an Englishman is briefly told. He is always very sick and very faint; and has an intolerable headache, morning, noon, and night.

In the ladies' car, there is no smoking of tobacco allowed. All gentlemen who have ladies with them, sit in this car; and it is usually very full. Before it, is the gentlemen's car; which is something narrower. As I had a window close to me yesterday which commanded this gentlemen's car, I looked at it pretty often, perforce. The flashes of saliva flew so perpetually and incessantly out of the windows all the way, that it looked as though they were ripping open feather-beds inside, and letting the wind dispose of the feathers. But this spitting is universal. In the courts of law, the judge has his spittoon on the bench, the counsel have theirs, the witness has his, the prisoner his, and the crier his. The jury are accommodated at the rate of three men to a spittoon (or spit-box as they call it here); and the spectators in the gallery are provided for, as so many men who in the course of nature expectorate without cessation. There are spit-boxes in every steamboat, bar-room, public dining-room, house of office, and place of general resort, no matter what it be. In the hospitals, the students are requested, by placard, to use the boxes provided for them, and not to spit upon the stairs. I have twice seen gentlemen, at evening parties in New York, turn aside when they were not engaged in conversation, and spit upon the drawing-room carpet. And in every bar-room and hotel passage the stone floor looks as if it were paved with open oysters – from the quantity of this kind of deposit which tesselates it all over . . .

8. A visit to the president

To Albany Fonblanque (a leading British journalist, editor of The Examiner) *from Washington, 12 March. The president in 1842 was a Whig, John Tyler, formerly governor of Virginia, who stepped up to president from vice-president in 1841 when President W. H. Harrison died in office.*

I arrived here on Wednesday night; and on Thursday morning was taken there by the Secretary to the Senate: a namesake of mine, whom "John Tyler" had dispatched to carry me to him for a private interview which is considered a greater compliment than the public audience. We entered a large hall, and rang a large bell – if I may judge from the size of the handle. Nobody answering the bell, we walked about on our own account, as divers other gentlemen (mostly with their hats on, and their hands in their pockets) were doing, very leisurely. Some of them had ladies with them to whom they were shewing the premises; others were lounging on the chairs and sofas; others, yawning and picking their teeth. The greater part of this assemblage were rather asserting their supremacy than doing anything else; as they had no particular business there, that anybody knew of. A few were eyeing the moveables as if to make quite sure that the President (who is not popular) hadn't made away with any of the furniture, or sold the fixtures for his private benefit.

After glancing at these loungers who were scattered over a pretty drawing room, furnished with blue and silver, opening upon a terrace with a beautiful prospect of the Potomac River and adjacent country – and a larger state room, not unlike the dining room at the Athenæum – we went up stairs into another chamber, where were the more favored visitors who were waiting for audiences. At sight of my conductor, a black in plain clothes and yellow slippers, who was moving noiselessly about, and whispering messages in the ears of the more impatient, made a sign of recognition and glided off to announce us.

There were some twenty men in the room. One, a tall, wiry muscular old man from the West, sunburnt and swarthy, – with a brown white hat and a giant umbrella, who sat bolt upright in his chair, frowning steadily at the carpet, as if he had made up his mind that he was going to "fix" the President in what he had to say, and wouldn't bate him a grain. Another, a Kentucky farmer nearly seven feet high, with his hat on, and his hands under his coat tails, who leaned against the wall, and kicked the floor with his heel, as though he had Time's head under his shoe, and were literally "killing" him. A third, a short, round-faced man with sleek black hair cropped close, and whiskers and beard shaved down into blue dots, who sucked the head of a big

"In the White House," from American Notes

President John Tyler

stick, and from time to time took it out of his mouth to see how it was getting on. A fourth did nothing but whistle. The rest balanced themselves, now on one leg, and now on the other, and chewed mighty quids of tobacco – such mighty quids, that they all looked as if their faces were swoln with erysipelas. They all constantly squirted forth upon the carpet, a yellow saliva which quite altered its pattern; and even the few who did not indulge in this recreation, expectorated abundantly.

In five minutes' time, the black in yellow slippers came back, and led us into an upper room – a kind of office – where, by the side of a hot stove, though it was a very hot day, sat the President – all alone; and close to him a great spit box, which is an indispensable article of furniture here. In the private sitting room in which I am writing this, there are two; one on each side of the fire place. They are made of brass, to match the fender and fire irons; and are as bright as decanter stands. – But I am wandering from the President. Well! The President got up, and said, "Is *this* Mr. Dickens?" – "Sir," returned Mr. Dickens – "it is". "I am astonished to see so young a man Sir", said the President. Mr. Dickens smiled, and thought of returning the compliment – but he didn't; for the President looked too worn and tired, to justify it. "I am happy to join with my fellow citizens in welcoming you, warmly, to this country", said the President. Mr. Dickens thanked him, and shook hands. Then the other Mr. Dickens, the secretary, asked the President to come to his house that night, which the President said he should be glad to do, but for the pressure of business, and measles. Then the President and the two Mr. Dickenses sat and looked at each other, until Mr. Dickens of London observed that no doubt the President's time was fully occupied, and he and the other Mr. Dickens had better go. Upon that they all rose up; and the President invited Mr. Dickens (of London) to come again, which he said he would. And that was the end of the conference.

The Senate in session

9. Congressmen

To Forster from Washington, 15 March. For details concerning the individual statesmen mentioned by Dickens see The Pilgrim Edition of the Letters of Charles Dickens, *ed. M. House, G. Storey, and K. Tillotson, vol. 3 (Oxford: Clarendon Press, 1974), pp. 134–135.*

I have the privilege of appearing on the floor of both houses here, and go to them every day. They are very handsome and commodious. There is a great deal of bad speaking, but there are a great many very remarkable men, in the legislature: such as John Quincey Adams, Clay, Preston, Calhoun, and others: with whom I need scarcely add I have been placed in the friendliest relations. Adams is a fine old fellow – seventy-six years old, but with most surprising vigour, memory, readiness, and pluck. Clay is perfectly enchanting; an irresistible man. There are some very noble specimens, too, out of the West. Splendid men to look at, hard to deceive, prompt to act, lions in energy, Crichtons in varied accomplishments, Indians in quickness of eye and gesture, Americans in affectionate and generous impulse. It would be difficult to exaggerate the nobility of some of these glorious fellows.

---

10. The American character

Continuation of the letter to Forster of 15 March.

I said I wouldn't write anything more concerning the American people, for two months. Second thoughts are best. I shall not change, and may as well speak out – to *you.* They are friendly, earnest, hospitable, kind, frank, very often accomplished, far less prejudiced than you would suppose, warm-hearted, fervent, and enthusiastic. They are chivalrous in their universal politeness to women, courteous, obliging, disinterested; and, when they conceive a perfect affection for a man (as I may venture to say of myself), entirely devoted to him. I have received thousands of people of all ranks and grades, and have never once been asked an offensive or unpolite question – except by Englishmen, who, when they have been "located" here for some years, are worse than the devil in his blackest painting. The State is a parent to its people; has a parental care and watch over all poor children, women labouring of child, sick persons, and captives. The common men render you assistance in the streets, and would revolt from the offer of a piece of money. The desire to oblige is universal; and I have never once travelled in a public conveyance, without making some generous acquaintance whom I have been sorry to part from, and who has in many cases come on miles, to see us again. But I don't like the country. I would not live here, on any consideration. It goes against the grain with me. It would with you. I think it impossible, utterly impossible, for any Englishman to live here, and be happy.

---

11. Slavery

To Forster from Washington, 21 March, after a visit to Richmond. Lord Ashburton was on his way to America to represent Britain in settling the northeast boundary dispute between the U.S. and Canada.

Richmond is a prettily situated town; but, like other towns in slave districts (as the planters themselves admit), has an aspect of decay and gloom which to an unaccustomed eye is *most* distressing. In the black car (for they don't let them sit with the whites), on the railroad as we went there, were a mother and family whom the steamer was conveying away, to sell; retaining the man (the husband and father I mean) on his plantation. The children cried the whole way. Yesterday, on board the boat, a slave owner and two constables were our fellow-passengers. They were coming here in search of two negroes who had run away on the previous day. On the bridge at Richmond there is a notice against fast driving over it, as it is rotten and crazy: penalty – for whites, five dollars; for slaves, fifteen stripes. My heart is lightened as if a great load had been taken from it, when I think that we are turning our backs on this accursed and detested system. I really don't think I could have borne it any longer. It is all very well to say "be silent on the subject." They won't let you be silent. They *will* ask you what you think of it; and *will* expatiate on slavery as if it were one of the greatest blessings of mankind. "It's not," said a hard, bad-looking fellow to me the other day, "it's not the interest of a man to use his slaves ill. It's damned nonsense that you hear in England." – I told him quietly that it was not a man's interest to get drunk, or to steal, or to game, or to indulge in any other vice, but he *did* indulge in it for all that. That cruelty, and the abuse of irresponsible power, were two of the bad passions of human nature, with the gratification of which, considerations of interest or of ruin had nothing whatever to do; and that, while every candid man must admit that even a slave might be

happy enough with a good master, all human beings knew that bad masters, cruel masters, and masters who disgraced the form they bore, were matters of experience and history, whose existence was as undisputed as that of slaves themselves. He was a little taken aback by this, and asked me if I believed in the bible. Yes, I said, but if any man could prove to me that it sanctioned slavery, I would place no further credence in it. "Well, then," he said, "by God, sir, the niggers must be kept down, and the whites have put down the coloured people wherever they have found them." "That's the whole question" said I. "Yes, and by God," says he, "the British had better not stand out on that point when Lord Ashburton comes over, for I never felt so warlike as I do now, – and that's a fact."

12. Further complaints of a Lion

Baltimore

To Daniel Maclise (painter and close friend of Dickens') from Baltimore, 22 March.

Imagine Kate and I – a kind of Queen and Albert – holding a Levee every day (proclaimed and placarded in newspapers) and receiving all who choose to come. Imagine – but you can't imagine, without seeing them – how now and then a republican boy, of surpassing and indescribable free and easiness comes in among the company, and keeping his cap upon his head, inspects me at his leisure. We had one the other day who remained two hours, and took no other refreshment during the whole time than an occasional pick at his nose, or survey of the street from the open window, whence he invited other boys to come up, and do the like. Imagine, when I landed from a steam boat in New York, in a dense crowd, some twenty or thirty people, screwing small dabs of fur out of the back of that costly great coat I bought in Regent Street! Imagine these public receptions occurring *every day*, and how I feel towards the people who come in, fresh, and full of speech and questioning, when I am quite tired out! Every railroad car is like a great omnibus. Whenever we come to a town station, the crowd surround it, let down all the windows, thrust in their heads, stare at me, and compare notes respecting my appearance, with as much coolness as if I were a marble image. What do you think of *that* – as you would say, yourself.

---

13. "Not the Republic of my imagination"

To W. C. Macready (the "Eminent Tragedian," much loved and admired by Dickens) from Baltimore, 22 March. Dickens mentions the King of Prussia because that monarch had just paid a state visit to England which had, of course, been extensively reported in the newspapers. George Bancroft was a Bostonian, a distinguished historian and diplomat; William Bryant was editor of the New York Evening Post.

This is not the Republic I came to see. This is not the Republic of my imagination. I infinitely prefer a liberal Monarchy – even with its sickening accomplishments of Court Circulars, and Kings of Prussia – to such a Government as this. In every respect but that of National Education, the Country disappoints me. The more I think of its youth and strength, the poorer and more trifling in a thousand respects, it appears in my eyes. In everything of which it has made a boast – excepting its education of the people, and its care for poor children – it sinks im-

measurably below the level I had placed it upon. And England, even England, bad and faulty as the old land is, and miserable as millions of her people are, rises in the comparison. Strike down the established church, and I would take her to my heart for better or worse, and reject this new love without a pang or moment's hesitation.

You live here, Macready, as I have sometimes heard you imagining! *You!* Loving you with all my heart and soul, and knowing what your disposition really is, I would not condemn you to a year's residence on this side of the Atlantic, for any money. Freedom of opinion! Where is it? I see a press more mean and paltry and silly and disgraceful than any country ever knew, – if that be its standard, here it is. But I speak of Bancroft, and am advised to be silent on that subject, for he is "a black sheep – a democrat". I speak of Bryant, and am entreated to be more careful – for the same reason. I speak of International copyright, and am implored not to ruin myself outright. I speak of Miss Martineau, and all parties – slave upholders and abolitionists; Whigs, Tyler Whigs, and Democrats, shower down upon her a perfect cataract of abuse. "But what has she done? Surely she praised America enough!" – "Yes, but she told us of some of our faults, and Americans can't bear to be told of their faults. Don't split on that rock, Mr. Dickens, don't write about America – we are so very suspicious." – Freedom of opinion! Macready, if I had been born here, and had written my books in this country, – producing them with no stamp of approval from any other land – it is my solemn belief that I should have lived and died, poor, unnoticed, and "a black sheep" – to boot. I never was more convinced of anything than I am of that.

---

14. A smart youngster

To Forster, 28 March. Written aboard a canal boat, journeying to Pittsburgh. Dickens had travelled from Baltimore to York, Pennsylvania, by rail and then by stagecoach to Harrisburg.

I think I formerly made a casual remark to you touching the precocity of the youth of this country. When we changed horses on this journey I got down to stretch my legs, refresh myself with a glass of whiskey and water, and shake the wet off my great coat – for it was raining very heavily, and continued to do so, all night. Mounting on my seat again, I observed something lying on the roof of the coach, which I took to be a rather large fiddle in a brown bag. In the course of ten miles or so, however, I discovered that it had a pair of dirty shoes at one end, and a glazed cap at the other; and further observation demonstrated it to be a small boy, in a snuff-coloured coat, with his arms quite pinioned to his sides by deep forcing into his pockets. He was, I presume, a relative or friend of the coachman's, as he lay a-top of the luggage, with his face towards the rain; and, except when a change of position brought his shoes in contact with my hat, he appeared to be asleep. Sir, when we stopped to water the horses, about two miles from Harrisburgh, this thing slowly upreared itself to the height of three foot eight, and fixing its eyes on me with a mingled expression of complacency, patronage, national independence, and sympathy for all outer barbarians and foreigners, said, in shrill piping accents, "Well now, stranger, I guess you find this, a'most like an English a'ternoon, – hey?" It is unnecessary to add that I thirsted for his blood.

---

15. Life on a canal boat

Continuation of the letter to Forster of 28 March.

And now I come to the Canal Boat. Bless your heart and soul, my dear fellow, – if you could only see us on board the canal boat! Let me think, for a moment, at what time of the day or night I should best like you to see us. In the morning? Between five and six in the morning, shall I say? Well! you *would* like to see me, standing on the deck, fishing the dirty water out of the canal with a tin ladle chained to the

Going to bed on an Erie packet

boat by a long chain; pouring the same into a tin-basin (also chained up in like manner); and scrubbing my face with the jack towel. At night, shall I say? I don't know that you *would* like to look into the cabin at night, only to see me lying on a temporary shelf exactly the width of this sheet of paper when it's open (*I measured it this morning*), with one man above me, and another below; and, in all, eight and twenty in a low cabin, which you can't stand upright in with your hat on. I don't think you would like to look in at breakfast time either, for then these shelves have only just been taken down and put away, and the atmosphere of the place is, as you may suppose, by no means fresh; though there *are* upon the table tea and coffee, and bread and butter, and salmon, and shad, and liver, and steak, and potatoes, and pickles, and ham, and pudding, and sausages; and three and thirty people sitting round it, eating and drinking; and savoury bottles of gin, and whiskey, and brandy, and rum, in the bar hard by; and seven and twenty out of the eight and twenty men, in foul linen, with yellow streams from half-chewed tobacco trickling down their chins. Perhaps the best time for you to take a peep would be the present: eleven o'clock in the forenoon: when the barber is at his shaving, and the gentlemen are lounging about the stove waiting for their turns, and not more than seventeen are spitting in concert, and two or three are walking overhead (lying down on the luggage every time the man at the helm calls "Bridge!"), and I am writing this in the ladies'-cabin, which is a part of the gentlemen's, and only screened off by a red curtain. Indeed it exactly resembles the dwarf's private apartment in a

Western end of the Erie Canal

caravan at a fair; and the gentlemen, generally, represent the spectators at a penny-a-head. The place is just as clean and just as large as
that caravan you and I were in at Greenwich-fair last past. Outside, it
is exactly like any canal-boat you have seen near the Regent's-park, or
elsewhere.

.   .   .   .

I am considered very hardy in the morning, for I run up, bare-necked,
and plunge my head into the half-frozen water, by half-past five
o'clock. I am respected for my activity, inasmuch as I jump from the
boat to the towing-path, and walk five or six miles before breakfast;
keeping up with the horses all the time. In a word, they are quite astonished to find a sedentary Englishman roughing it so well, and taking so much exercise; and question me very much on that head. The
greater part of the men will sit and shiver round the stove all day,
rather than put one foot before the other. As to having a window
open, that's not to be thought of.

16. A depressing landscape

*Continuation of the letter to Forster of 28 March. The mountains
Dickens refers to here are the Alleghenies. Glencoe is a sombre,
powerfully atmospheric valley in Scotland, the scene of a frightful
massacre in 1692.*

The scenery, before you reach the mountains, and when you are on
them, and after you have left them, is very grand and fine; and the
canal winds its way through some deep, sullen gorges, which, seen by
moonlight, are very impressive: though immeasurably inferior to
Glencoe, to whose terrors I have not seen the smallest *approach*. We
have passed, both in the mountains and elsewhere, a great number of
new settlements, and detached log-houses. Their utterly forlorn and
miserable appearance baffles all description. I have not seen six cabins
out of six hundred, where the windows have been whole. Old hats,
old clothes, old boards, old fragments of blanket and paper, are stuffed
into the broken glass; and their air is misery and desolation. It pains
the eye to see the stumps of great trees thickly strewn in every field
of wheat; and never to lose the eternal swamp and dull morass, with
hundreds of rotten trunks, of elm and pine and sycamore and log-
wood, steeped in its unwholesome water; where the frogs so croak at

night that after dark there is an incessant sound as if millions of phantom teams, with bells, were travelling through the upper air, at an enormous distance off. It is quite an oppressive circumstance, too, to *come* upon great tracks, where settlers have been burning down the trees; and where their wounded bodies lie about, like those of murdered creatures; while here and there some charred and blackened giant rears two bare arms aloft, and seems to curse his enemies. The prettiest sight I have seen was yesterday, when we – on the heights of the mountain, and in a keen wind – looked down into a valley full of light and softness: catching glimpses of scattered cabins; children running to the doors; dogs bursting out to bark; pigs scampering home, like so many prodigal sons; families sitting out in their gardens; cows gazing upward, with a stupid indifference; men in their shirt-sleeves looking on at their unfinished houses, and planning work for to-morrow; – and the train riding on, high above them, like a storm.

---

17. "Fixing" the Queen's English

Continuation of the letter to Forster of 28 March. "Mr. Q" was George Washington Putnam, whom Dickens had hired to act as his secretary during his American tour.

I told you of the many uses of the word "fix." I ask Mr. Q on board a steamboat if breakfast be nearly ready, and he tells me yes he should think so, for when he was last below the steward was "fixing the tables" – in other words, laying the cloth. When we have been writing, and I beg him (do you remember anything of my love of order, at this distance of time?) to collect our papers, he answers that he'll "fix 'em presently." So when a man's dressing he's "fixing" himself, and when you put yourself under a doctor he "fixes" you in no time. T'other night, before we came on board here, when I had ordered a bottle of mulled claret and waited some time for it, it was put on table with an apology from the landlord (a lieutenant-colonel) that "he fear'd it wasn't fixed properly." And here, on Saturday morning, a Western man, handing the potatoes to Mr. Q at breakfast, enquired if he wouldn't take some of "these fixings" with his meat. I remained as grave as a judge. I catch them looking at me sometimes, and feel that they think I don't take any notice.

---

18. A diseased body politic

To W. C. Macready, 1 April, on board the steamboat from Pittsburgh to Cincinnati. For "Lord Ashburton's appointment" see the headnote to extract 11.

I have said to Forster that I believe the heaviest blow ever dealt at Liberty's Head, will be dealt by this nation in the ultimate failure of its example to the Earth. See what is passing now – Look at the exhausted Treasury; the paralyzed government; the unworthy representatives of a free people; the desperate contests between the North and the South; the iron curb and brazen muzzle fastened upon every man who speaks his mind, even in that Republican Hall, to which Republican men are sent by a Republican people to speak Republican Truths – the stabbings, and shootings, and coarse and brutal threatenings exchanged between Senators under the very Senate's roof – the intrusion of the most pitiful, mean, malicious, creeping, crawling, sneaking party spirit, into all transactions of life – even into the appointments of physicians to pauper madhouses – the silly, drivelling, slanderous, wicked, monstrous Party Press. I say nothing of the egotism which makes of Lord Ashburton's appointment, the conciliatory act of a frightened Government; nothing of the boastful, vain-glorious spirit which dictates a million of such absurdities; and which is *not English*. I love and honor very many of the people here – but *"the Mass"* (to use our monarchical term) are miserably dependent in great things, and miserably independent in small ones. That's a Truth, and you will find it so. The Nation is a body without a head; and the arms and legs, are occupied in quarrelling with the trunk and each other, and exchanging bruises at random.

---

19. Bores

To Forster, 1 April, on board the steamboat from Pittsburgh to Cincinnati. Phrenology was a very popular Victorian pseudoscience; people's characters, it was believed, could be ascertained by examining the shape of their skulls. The abbreviation "LL" stands for "Literary Lady" (see extract 68).

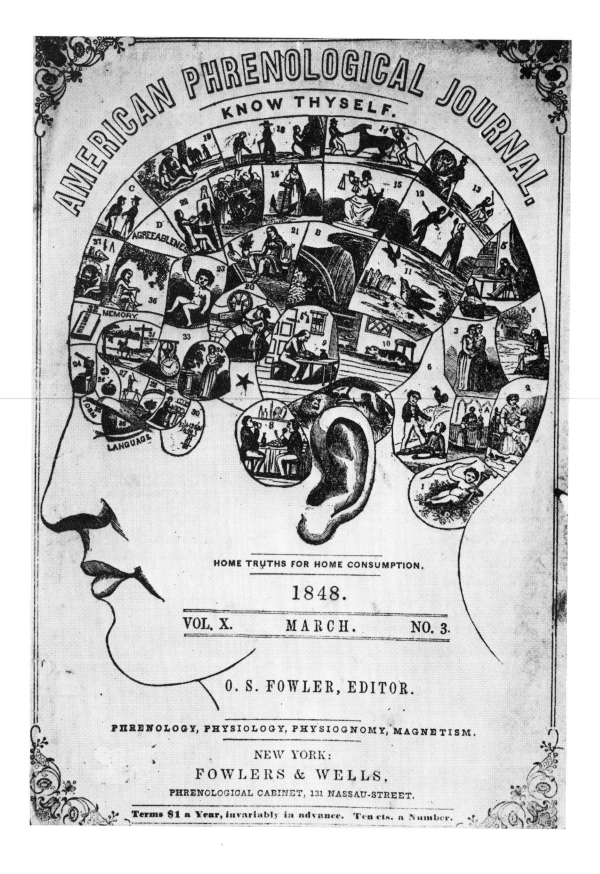

AMERICAN PHRENOLOGICAL JOURNAL.

KNOW THYSELF.

HOME TRUTHS FOR HOME CONSUMPTION.

1848.

VOL. X.   MARCH.   NO. 3.

O. S. FOWLER, EDITOR.

PHRENOLOGY, PHYSIOLOGY, PHYSIOGNOMY, MAGNETISM.

NEW YORK:

FOWLERS & WELLS,

PHRENOLOGICAL CABINET, 131 NASSAU-STREET.

Terms $1 a Year, invariably in advance. Ten cts. a Number.

My friend the New Englander, of whom I wrote last night, is per-haps the most intolerable bore on this vast continent. He drones, and snuffles, and writes poems, and talks small philosophy and meta-physics, and never *will* be quiet, under any circumstances. He is going to a great temperance convention at Cincinnati; along with a doctor of whom I saw something at Pittsburgh. The doctor, in addition to being everything that the New Englander is, is a phrenologist besides. I dodge them about the boat. Whenever I appear on deck, I see them bearing down upon me – and fly. The New Englander was very anx-ious last night that he and I should "form a magnetic chain," and magnetize the doctor, for the benefit of all incredulous passengers; but I declined, on the plea of tremendous occupation in the way of letter-writing.

. . . .

Besides the doctor and the dread New Englander, we have on board that valiant general who wrote to me about the "two LL's." He is an old, old man with a weazen face, and the remains of a pigeon-breast in his military surtout. He is acutely gentlemanly and officer-like. The breast has so subsided, and the face has become so strongly marked, that he seems, like a pigeon-pie, to show only the feet of the bird out-side, and to keep the rest to himself. He is perhaps *the* most horrible bore in this country. And I am quite serious when I say that I do not believe there are, on the whole earth besides, so many intensified bores as in these United States. No man can form an adequate idea of the real meaning of the word, without coming here.

Symbolical head

Pages 100–101
Cincinnati

---

20. A Cincinnati temperance festival

To Forster, 15 April. Returning from St. Louis to Cincinnati on board the steamboat Messenger. *Father Mathew was a very celebrated and successful preacher of temperance in Ireland from 1838.*

Cincinnati is only fifty years old, but is a very beautiful city: I think the prettiest place I have seen here, except Boston. It has risen out of the forest like an Arabian-night city; is well laid out; ornamented in the suburbs with pretty villas; and above all, for this is a very rare fea-ture in America, has smooth turf-plots and well-kept gardens. There happened to be a great temperance festival; and the procession mus-

tered under, and passed, our windows early in the morning. I suppose they were twenty thousand strong, at least. Some of the banners were quaint and odd enough. The ship-carpenters, for instance, displayed on one side of their flag, the good Ship Temperance in full sail; on the other, the Steamer Alcohol blowing up sky-high. The Irishmen had a portrait of Father Mathew, you may be sure. And Washington's broad lower jaw (by the bye, Washington had not a pleasant face) figured in all parts of the ranks. In a kind of square at one outskirt of the city, they divided into bodies, and were addressed by different speakers. Drier speaking I never heard. I own that I felt quite uncomfortable to think they could take the taste of it out of their mouths with nothing better than water.

---

21. On the Mississippi

Continuation of the letter to Forster of 15 April.

The last 200 miles of the voyage from Cincinnati to St. Louis are upon the Mississippi, for you come down the Ohio to its mouth. It is well for society that this Mississippi, the renowned father of waters, had no children who take after him. It is the beastliest river in the world. . . .

Conceive the pleasure of rushing down this stream by night (as we did last night) at the rate of fifteen miles an hour; striking against floating blocks of timber every instant; and dreading some infernal

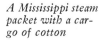

A Mississippi steam packet with a cargo of cotton

A MISSISSIPPI STEAMER.

blow at every bump. The helmsman in these boats is in a little glass-house upon the roof. In the Mississippi, another man stands in the very head of the vessel, listening and watching intently; listening, because they can tell in dark nights by the noise when any great obstruction is at hand. This man holds the rope of a large bell which hangs close to the wheel-house, and whenever he pulls it, the engine is to stop directly, and not to stir until he rings again. Last night, this bell rang at least once in every five minutes; and at each alarm there was a concussion which nearly flung one out of bed. . . . While I have been writing this account, we have shot out of that hideous river, thanks be to God; never to see it again, I hope, but in a nightmare. We are now on the smooth Ohio, and the change is like the transition from pain to perfect ease.

---

22. Slavery and its defenders

Continuation of the letter to Forster of 15 April. The "pretty vignette" was a newspaper advertisement headed "Runaway Negro in Jail." Dr. Bartlett was professor of medicine at Transylvania University in Lexington, Kentucky.

It is not six years ago, since a slave in this very same St. Louis, being arrested (I forget for what), and knowing he had no chance of a fair trial be his offence what it might, drew his bowie knife and ripped the constable across the body. A scuffle ensuing, the desperate negro stabbed two others with the same weapon. The mob who gathered round (among whom were men of mark, wealth, and influence in the place) overpowered him by numbers; carried him away to a piece of open ground beyond the city; *and burned him alive.* This, I say, was done within six years in broad day; in a city with its courts, lawyers, tipstaffs, judges, jails, and hangman; and not a hair on the head of one of those men has been hurt to this day. And it is, believe me, it is the miserable, wretched independence in small things; the paltry republicanism which recoils from honest service to an honest man, but does not shrink from every trick, artifice, and knavery in business; that makes these slaves necessary, and will render them so, until the indignation of other countries sets them free.

They say the slaves are fond of their masters. Look at this pretty vignette (part of the stock-in-trade of a newspaper), and judge how you would feel, when men, looking in your face, told you such tales

*Advertisements for
the apprehension
of runaway slaves,
from the appendix
to Frederick Law
Olmsted's A Jour-
ney through Texas*

$100 REWARD.

I WILL give the above reward for my boy BILL, who ran away on the 7th instant, from my plantation in Walker County, if taken up by any person west of the San Antonio River; fifty dollars, if taken up west of the Brazos; and twenty-five dollars to any person taking him up east of the Brazos River. The above reward will be paid on delivering said boy into the hands of any jailer convenient to where taken up, and who can securely keep him until I can get him.

BILL is what would be called a bright mulatto, of rather dull expression of countenance; his hair might be called straight, and, when long, very bushy. Was very long when he left home. His age is about 28 years; his height 5 feet 10 inches.

Took with him from home a double-barrel shot-gun.

WM. B. SCOTT.

Huntsville, April 14, 1855.

———

SEE the advertisement of W. B. Scott for his runaway negro, Bill. The fellow knocked down the overseer, and then ran to the house, got a gun, and put out before the overseer could overhaul him. Gen. Scott is anxious to recover the boy, in order to punish his insubordination.

———

TAKEN UP

AND committed to the jail of Bexar County, Texas, on the 13th day of March, 1854, a negro man, calling himself MARTIN, or TOM. He says he is a blacksmith, and belongs to John Beal, Attakapas, on Red River. Said negro is about 48 years of age, 5 feet 8 or 9 inches high, and head a little bald. His back is marked with the whip, and marks of cupping on both temples and back of the neck. He speaks Creole French and broken English. The owner of said negro is hereby notified to come forward, prove property, pay charges, and take him away, or he will be dealt with as the law directs.

W. B. KNOX, Sheriff B. C.

By L. SARGENT, Deputy.

———

with the newspaper lying on the table. In all the slave districts, advertisements for runaways are as much matters of course as the announcement of the play for the evening with us. The poor creatures themselves fairly worship English people: they would do anything for them. They are perfectly acquainted with all that takes place in reference to emancipation; and *of course* their attachment to us grows out of their deep devotion to their owners. I cut this illustration out of a newspaper which had a leader in reference to *the abominable and hellish doctrine of Abolition – repugnant alike to every law of God and Nature.* "I know something," said a Dr. Bartlett (a very accomplished man), late a fellow-passenger of ours: "I know something of their fondness for their masters. I live in Kentucky; and I can assert upon my honour, that, in my neighbourhood, it is as common for a runaway slave, retaken, to draw his bowie knife and rip his owner's bowels open, as it is for you to see a drunken fight in London."

23. The prairie

Continuation of the letter to Forster of 15 April. Captain Basil Hall,
R.N., had visited America in 1827/28 and published his Travels
in North America *in 1829. The American artist George Catlin had*
exhibited an "Indian Gallery" in London in 1840. Salisbury Plain
in Wiltshire, England, is the site of Stonehenge.

Now, a prairie is undoubtedly worth seeing – but more that one may
say one has seen it, than for any sublimity it possesses in itself. Like
most things, great or small, in this country, you hear of it with considerable exaggerations. Basil Hall was really quite right in depreciating
the general character of the scenery. The widely-famed Far West is
not to be compared with even the tamest portions of Scotland or
Wales. You stand upon the prairie, and see the unbroken horizon all
round you. You are on a great plain, which is like a sea without water.
I am exceedingly fond of wild and lonely scenery, and believe that I
have the faculty of being as much impressed by it as any man living.
But the prairie fell, by far, short of my preconceived idea. I felt no
such emotions as I do in crossing Salisbury plain. The excessive flatness
of the scene makes it dreary, but tame. Grandeur is certainly not its
characteristic. I retired from the rest of the party, to understand my

Red Buttes, Lara-
mie Plains

own feelings the better; and looked all round, again and again. It was fine. It was worth the ride. The sun was going down, very red and bright; and the prospect looked like that ruddy sketch of Catlin's, which attracted our attention (you remember?); except that there was not so much ground as he represents, between the spectator and the horizon. But to say (as the fashion is, here) that the sight is a landmark in one's existence, and awakens a new set of sensations, is sheer gammon. I would say to every man who can't see a prairie – go to Salisbury plain, Marlborough downs, or any of the broad, high, open lands near the sea. Many of them are fully as impressive; and Salisbury plain is *decidedly* more so.

St. Louis

24. St. Louis society

Continuation of the letter to Forster of 15 April.

The inns in these outlandish corners of the world would astonish you by their goodness. The Planter's-house is as large as the Middlesex-hospital and built very much on our hospital plan, with long wards abundantly ventilated, and plain whitewashed walls. They had a famous notion of sending up at breakfast-time large glasses of new milk with blocks of ice in them as clear as crystal. Our table was abundantly supplied indeed at every meal. One day when Kate and I were din-

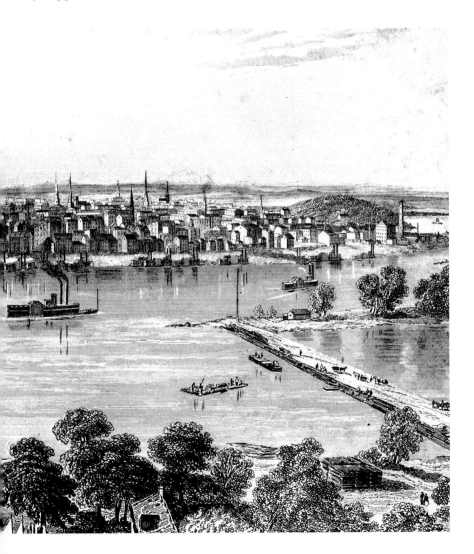

ing alone together, in our own room, we counted sixteen dishes on the table at the same time.

The society is pretty rough, and intolerably conceited. All the inhabitants are young. *I didn't see one grey head in St. Louis.* There is an island close by, called bloody island. It is the duelling ground of St. Louis; and is so called from the last fatal duel which was fought there. It was a pistol duel, breast to breast, and both parties fell dead at the same time. One of our prairie party (a young man) had acted there as second in several encounters. The last occasion was a duel with rifles, at forty paces; and coming home he told us how he had bought his man a coat of green linen to fight in, woollen being usually fatal to rifle wounds.

---

25. A corduroy road

To Forster from Sandusky, 24 April. The uncomfortable road Dickens is describing was between Columbus and Sandusky.

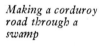

Making a corduroy road through a swamp

It is impossible to convey an adequate idea to you of the kind of road over which we travelled. I can only say that it was, at the best, but a track through the wild forest, and among the swamps, bogs, and morasses of the withered bush. A great portion of it was what is called a "corduroy road:" which is made by throwing round logs or whole trees into a swamp, and leaving them to settle there. Good Heaven! if you only felt one of the least of the jolts with which the coach falls from log to log! It is like nothing but going up a steep flight of stairs in an omnibus. . . . Still, the day was beautiful, the air delicious, and we were *alone*: with no tobacco spittle, or eternal prosy conversation about dollars and politics (the only two subjects they ever converse about, or can converse upon) to bore us.

---

26. Midwestern manners

Continuation of the letter to Forster of 24 April. The people Dickens refers to in the first two sentences are the Wyandot Indians.

They are a fine people, but degraded and broken down. If you could see any of their men and women on a race-course in England, you would not know them from gipsies.

We are in a small house here, but a very comfortable one, and the people are exceedingly obliging. Their demeanour in these country parts is invariably morose, sullen, clownish, and repulsive. I should think there is not, on the face of the earth, a people so entirely destitute of humour, vivacity, or the capacity of enjoyment. It is most remarkable. I am quite serious when I say that I have not heard a hearty laugh these six weeks, except my own; nor have I seen a merry face on any shoulders but a black man's. Lounging listlessly about, idling in bar-rooms; smoking; spitting; and lolling on the pavement in rocking-chairs, outside the shop doors; are the only recreations. I don't think the national shrewdness extends beyond the Yankees; that is, the Eastern men. The rest are heavy, dull, and ignorant. Our landlord here is from the East. He is a handsome, obliging, civil fellow. He comes into the room with his hat on; spits in the fire place as he talks; sits down on the sofa with his hat on; pulls out his newspaper, and reads; but to all this I am accustomed. He is anxious to please – and that is enough.

---

27. International copyright again

To Forster from Niagara Falls, 3 May.

I'll tell you what the two obstacles to the passing of an international copyright law with England, are: firstly, the national love of "doing" a man in any bargain or matter of business; secondly, the national vanity. Both these characteristics prevail to an extent which no stranger can possibly estimate.

With regard to the first, I seriously believe that it is an essential part of the pleasure derived from the perusal of a popular English book, that the author gets nothing for it. It is so dar-nation 'cute – so knowing in Jonathan to get his reading on those terms. He has the Englishman so regularly on the hip that his eye twinkles with slyness, cunning, and delight; and he chuckles over the humour of the page with an appreciation of it, quite inconsistent with, and apart from, its honest purchase. The raven hasn't more joy in eating a stolen piece of meat, than the American has in reading the English book which he gets for nothing.

With regard to the second, it reconciles that better and more elevated class who are above this sort of satisfaction, with surprising ease. The man's read in America! The Americans like him! They are glad to see him when he comes here! They flock about him, and tell him that they are grateful to him for spirits in sickness; for many hours of delight in health; for a hundred fanciful associations which are constantly interchanged between themselves and their wives and children at home! It is nothing that all this takes place in countries where he is *paid*: it is nothing that he has won fame for himself elsewhere, and profit too. The Americans read him; the free, enlightened, independent Americans; and what more *would* he have? Here's reward enough for any man. The national vanity swallows up all other countries on the face of the earth, and leaves but this above the ocean. Now, mark what the real value of this American reading is. Find me in the whole range of literature one single solitary English book which becomes popular with them, before it has forced itself on their attention by going through the ordeal at home and becoming popular there – and I am content that the law should remain as it is, for ever and a day. I must make one exception. There *are* some mawkish tales of fashionable life before which crowds fall down as they were gilded calves, which at home have been snugly enshrined in circulating libraries from the date of their publication.

As to telling them they will have no literature of their own, the

universal answer (out of Boston) is, "We don't want one. Why should we pay for one when we can get it for nothing? Our people don't think of poetry, sir. Dollars, banks, and cotton are *our* books, sir." And they certainly are in one sense; for a lower average of general information than exists in this country on all other topics, it would be very hard to find. So much, at present, for international copyright.

II. *American Notes*

CITIES

28. Boston

CHAPTER 3

Harlequin and Columbine are characters from the Italian commedia dell'arte *who were imported into English pantomime.*

When I got into the streets upon this Sunday morning, the air was so clear, the houses were so bright and gay; the signboards were painted in such gaudy colours; the gilded letters were so very golden; the bricks were so very red, the stone was so very white, the blinds and area railings were so very green, the knobs and plates upon the street doors so marvellously bright and twinkling; and all so slight and un-substantial in appearance – that every thoroughfare in the city looked exactly like a scene in a pantomime. It rarely happens in the business streets that a tradesman, if I may venture to call anybody a tradesman, where everybody is a merchant, resides above his store; so that many occupations are often carried on in one house, and the whole front is covered with boards and inscriptions. As I walked along, I kept glanc-ing up at these boards, confidently expecting to see a few of them change into something; and I never turned a corner suddenly without looking out for the clown and pantaloon, who, I had no doubt, were hiding in a doorway or behind some pillar close at hand. As to Harle-quin and Columbine, I discovered immediately that they lodged (they are always looking after lodgings in a pantomime) at a very small clockmaker's one story high, near the hotel; which, in addition to vari-ous symbols and devices, almost covering the whole front, had a great dial hanging out – to be jumped through, of course.

The suburbs are, if possible, even more unsubstantial-looking than the city. The white wooden houses (so white that it makes one wink to look at them), with their green jalousie blinds, are so sprinkled and dropped about in all directions, without seeming to have any root at all in the ground; and the small churches and chapels are so prim, and bright, and highly varnished; that I almost believed the whole affair could be taken up piecemeal like a child's toy, and crammed into a little box.

The city is a beautiful one, and cannot fail, I should imagine, to im-press all strangers very favourably. The private dwelling-houses are, for the most part, large and elegant; the shops extremely good; and the public buildings handsome. The State House is built upon the

Boston Common

summit of a hill, which rises gradually at first, and afterwards by a steep ascent, almost from the water's edge. In front is a green enclosure, called the Common. The site is beautiful: and from the top there is a charming panoramic view of the whole town and neighbourhood. In addition to a variety of commodious offices, it contains two handsome chambers; in one the House of Representatives of the State hold their meetings: in the other, the Senate. Such proceedings as I saw here, were conducted with perfect gravity and decorum; and were certainly calculated to inspire attention and respect.

A westerly view of Harvard University, Cambridge

There is no doubt that much of the intellectual refinement and superiority of Boston is referable to the quiet influence of the University of Cambridge, which is within three or four miles of the city. The resident professors at that university are gentlemen of learning and varied attainments; and are, without one exception that I can call to mind, men who would shed a grace upon, and do honour to, any society in the civilised world. Many of the resident gentry in Boston and its neighbourhood, and I think I am not mistaken in adding, a large majority of those who are attached to the liberal professions there, have been educated at this same school. Whatever the defects of American universities may be, they disseminate no prejudices; rear no bigots; dig up the buried ashes of no old superstitions; never interpose between the people and their improvement; exclude no man because of his religious opinions; above all, in their whole course of study and instruction, recognise a world, and a broad one too, lying beyond the college walls.

It was a source of inexpressible pleasure to me to observe the almost imperceptible, but not less certain effect, wrought by this institution among the small community of Boston; and to note at every turn the humanising tastes and desires it has engendered; the affectionate friendships to which it has given rise; the amount of vanity and prejudice it has dispelled. The golden calf they worship at Boston is a pigmy compared with the giant effigies set up in other parts of that vast counting-house which lies beyond the Atlantic; and the almighty dollar sinks into something comparatively insignificant, amidst a whole Pantheon of better gods.

---

29. New York: Wall Street

CHAPTER 6

Lombard Street, named after the Lombardy merchants resident there in the Middle Ages, is the main street of London's financial district.

This narrow thoroughfare, baking and blistering in the sun, is Wall Street: the Stock Exchange and Lombard Street of New York. Many a rapid fortune has been made in this street, and many a no less rapid ruin. Some of these very merchants whom you see hanging about here now, have locked up money in their strong-boxes, like the man in the Arabian Nights, and opening them again, have found but withered leaves. Below, here by the water-side, where the bowsprits of ships stretch across the footway, and almost thrust themselves into the windows, lie the noble American vessels which have made their Packet Service the finest in the world. They have brought hither the foreigners who abound in all the streets: not, perhaps, that there are more here, than in other commercial cities; but elsewhere, they have particular haunts, and you must find them out; here, they pervade the town.

---

30. New York: the Five Points

CHAPTER 6

The name of Almack's is taken from that of a famous assembly room in St. James's, London. A "Jim Crow" act was an extravagant dance involving much jumping and spinning around, performed either by an actual black man or a white man made up as a black.

We have seen no beggars in the streets by night or day; but of other kinds of strollers, plenty. Poverty, wretchedness, and vice, are rife enough where we are going now.

This is the place: these narrow ways, diverging to the right and left,

Wall Street

The Five Points

and reeking everywhere with dirt and filth. Such lives as are led here, bear the same fruits here as elsewhere. The coarse and bloated faces at the doors, have counterparts at home, and all the wide world over. Debauchery has made the very houses prematurely old. See how the rotten beams are tumbling down, and how the patched and broken windows seem to scowl dimly, like eyes that have been hurt in drunken frays. Many of those pigs live here. Do they ever wonder why their masters walk upright in lieu of going on all-fours? and why they talk instead of grunting?

So far, nearly every house is a low tavern; and on the bar-room walls, are coloured prints of Washington, and Queen Victoria of England, and the American Eagle. Among the pigeon-holes that hold the bottles, are pieces of plate-glass and coloured paper, for there is, in some sort, a taste for decoration, even here. And as seamen frequent these haunts, there are maritime pictures by the dozen: of partings between sailors and their lady-loves, portraits of William, of the ballad, and his Black-Eyed Susan; of Will Watch, the Bold Smuggler; of Paul Jones the Pirate, and the like: on which the painted eyes of Queen Victoria, and of Washington to boot, rest in as strange companionship, as on most of the scenes that are enacted in their wondering presence.

What place is this, to which the squalid street conducts us? A kind of square of leprous houses, some of which are attainable only by crazy wooden stairs without. What lies beyond this tottering flight of steps, that creak beneath our tread? – a miserable room, lighted by one dim candle, and destitute of all comfort, save that which may be hidden in a wretched bed. Beside it, sits a man: his elbows on his knees: his forehead hidden in his hands. "What ails that man?" asks the foremost officer. "Fever," he sullenly replies, without looking up. Conceive the fancies of a feverish brain, in such a place as this!

Ascend these pitch-dark stairs, heedful of a false footing on the trembling boards, and grope your way with me into this wolfish den, where neither ray of light nor breath of air, appears to come. A negro lad, startled from his sleep by the officer's voice – he knows it well – but comforted by his assurance that he has not come on business, officiously bestirs himself to light a candle. The match flickers for a moment, and shows great mounds of dusty rags upon the ground: then dies away and leaves a denser darkness than before, if there can be degrees in such extremes. He stumbles down the stairs and presently comes back, shading a flaring taper with his hand. Then the mounds of rags are seen to be astir, and rise slowly up, and the floor is covered with heaps of negro women, waking from their sleep: their white teeth chattering, and their bright eyes glistening and winking on all sides with surprise and fear, like the countless repetition of one astonished African face in some strange mirror.

Mount up these other stairs with no less caution (there are traps and pitfalls here, for those who are not so well escorted as ourselves) into the housetop; where the bare beams and rafters meet overhead, and calm night looks down through the crevices in the roof. Open the door of one of these cramped hutches full of sleeping negroes. Pah! They have a charcoal fire within; there is a smell of singeing clothes, or flesh, so close they gather round the brazier; and vapours issue forth that blind and suffocate. From every corner, as you glance about you in these dark retreats, some figure crawls half-awakened, as if the judgment-hour were near at hand, and every obscene grave were giving up its dead. Where dogs would howl to lie, women, and men, and boys slink off to sleep, forcing the dislodged rats to move away in quest of better lodgings.

Here too are lanes and alleys, paved with mud knee-deep, underground chambers, where they dance and game; the walls bedecked with rough designs of ships, and forts, and flags, and American eagles out of number: ruined houses, open to the street, whence, through wide gaps in the walls, other ruins loom upon the eye, as though the world of vice and misery had nothing else to show: hideous tenements which take their name from robbery and murder: all that is loathsome, drooping, and decayed is here.

Our leader has his hand upon the latch of "Almack's," and calls to us from the bottom of the steps; for the assembly-room of the Five Point fashionables is approached by a descent. Shall we go in? It is but a moment.

Heyday! the landlady of Almack's thrives! A buxom fat mulatto woman, with sparkling eyes, whose head is daintily ornamented with a handkerchief of many colours. Nor is the landlord much behind her in his finery, being attired in a smart blue jacket, like a ship's steward, with a thick gold ring upon his little finger, and round his neck a gleaming golden watch-guard. How glad he is to see us! What will we please to call for? A dance? It shall be done directly, Sir: "a regular break-down."

The corpulent black fiddler, and his friend who plays the tambourine, stamp upon the boarding of the small raised orchestra in which they sit, and play a lively measure. Five or six couples come upon the floor, marshalled by a lively young negro, who is the wit of the assembly, and the greatest dancer known. He never leaves off making queer faces, and is the delight of all the rest, who grin from ear to ear incessantly. Among the dancers are two young mulatto girls, with large, black, drooping eyes, and head-gear after the fashion of the hostess, who are as shy, or feign to be, as though they never danced before, and so look down before the visitors, that their partners can see nothing but the long fringed lashes.

But the dance commences. Every gentleman sets as long as he likes to the opposite lady, and the opposite lady to him, and all are so long about it that the sport begins to languish, when suddenly the lively hero dashes in to the rescue. Instantly the fiddler grins, and goes at it tooth and nail; there is new energy in the tambourine; new laughter in the dancers; new smiles in the landlady; new confidence in the landlord; new brightness in the very candles. Single shuffle, double shuffle, cut and cross-cut; snapping his fingers, rolling his eyes, turning in his knees, presenting the backs of his legs in front, spinning about on his toes and heels like nothing but the man's fingers on the tambourine; dancing with two left legs, two right legs, two wooden legs, two wire legs, two spring legs – all sorts of legs and no legs – what is this to him? And in what walk of life, or dance of life, does man ever get such stimulating applause as thunders about him, when, having danced his partner off her feet, and himself too, he finishes by leaping gloriously on the bar-counter, and calling for something to drink, with the chuckle of a million of counterfeit Jim Crows, in one inimitable sound!

31. Philadelphia

CHAPTER 7

The two painters mentioned by Dickens are Philadelphia-born Benjamin West (1738–1820), who settled in London in 1763, and English-born Thomas Sully (1783–1872), who settled in Philadelphia. The allusion to Goldsmith's Vicar of Wakefield *refers to chapter 9 of that novel (a favourite of Dickens'), where some ladies refuse to talk of anything "but high life and high-lived company: with other fashionable topics, such as pictures, taste, Shakespeare, and the musical glasses." Girard College was at last finished; it became a school for white orphan boys.*

It is a handsome city, but distractingly regular. After walking about it for an hour or two, I felt that I would have given the world for a crooked street. The collar of my coat appeared to stiffen, and the brim of my hat to expand, beneath its quakery influence. My hair shrunk into a sleek short crop, my hands folded themselves upon my breast of their own calm accord, and thoughts of taking lodgings in Mark Lane over against the Market Place, and of making a large fortune by speculations in corn, came over me involuntarily.

Philadelphia is most bountifully provided with fresh water, which is showered and jerked about, and turned on, and poured off, every-

Market Street, looking down from Sixth Street.

Girard College.

Arch Street, looking up.

Philadelphia, from Independence Hall, looking east.

Chestnut Street, looking up from Independence Hall.

Chestnut Street, looking down from Ninth Street.

where. The Waterworks, which are on a height near the city, are no less ornamental than useful, being tastefully laid out as a public garden, and kept in the best and neatest order. The river is dammed at this point, and forced by its own power into certain high tanks or reservoirs, whence the whole city, to the top stories of the houses, is supplied at a very trifling expense. *Scenes in Philadelphia*

There are various public institutions. Among them a most excellent Hospital – a quaker establishment, but not sectarian in the great benefits it confers; a quiet, quaint old Library, named after Franklin; a handsome Exchange and Post Office; and so forth. In connexion with the quaker Hospital, there is a picture by West, which is exhibited for the benefit of the funds of the institution. The subject is, our Saviour healing the sick, and it is, perhaps, as favourable a specimen of the master as can be seen anywhere. Whether this be high or low praise, depends upon the reader's taste.

In the same room, there is a very characteristic and lifelike portrait by Mr. Sully, a distinguished American artist.

My stay in Philadelphia was very short, but what I saw of its society, I greatly liked. Treating of its general characteristics, I should be disposed to say that it is more provincial than Boston or New York, and that there is afloat in the fair city, an assumption of taste and criticism, savouring rather of those genteel discussions upon the same themes, in connexion with Shakespeare and the Musical Glasses, of which we read in the Vicar of Wakefield. Near the city, is a most splendid unfinished marble structure for the Girard College, founded by a deceased gentleman of that name and of enormous wealth, which, if completed according to the original design, will be perhaps the richest edifice of modern times. But the bequest is involved in legal disputes, and pending them the work has stopped; so that like many other great undertakings in America, even this is rather going to be done one of these days, than doing now.

---

32. Washington

CHAPTER 8

Pentonville is a northern suburb of London, described in 1833 as "melancholy and cut up with ... unoccupied rows of houses run up during the paroxysm of the brick and mortar mania of times past, and now tumbling in ruins." The City Road, celebrated for its taverns, connected Islington with the city of London. St. John's Wood was a rapidly developing, middle-class, northwestern suburb of London.

The *"aspiring Frenchman" was Pierre L'Enfant (1754–1825). The phrase "a Barmecide Feast" derives from a story in* The Arabian Nights *where a beggar is served an imaginary banquet in empty dishes.*

Take the worst parts of the City Road and Pentonville, or the straggling outskirts of Paris, where the houses are smallest, preserving all their oddities, but especially the small shops and dwellings, occupied in Pentonville (but not in Washington) by furniture-brokers, keepers of poor eating-houses, and fanciers of birds. Burn the whole down; build it up again in wood and plaster; widen it a little; throw in part of St. John's Wood; put green blinds outside all the private houses, with a red curtain and a white one in every window; plough up all the roads; plant a great deal of coarse turf in every place where it ought *not* to be; erect three handsome buildings in stone and marble, anywhere, but the more entirely out of everybody's way the better; call one the Post Office, one the Patent Office, and one the Treasury; make it scorching hot in the morning, and freezing cold in the afternoon, with an occasional tornado of wind and dust; leave a brick-field without the bricks, in all central places where a street may naturally be expected; and that's Washington.

It is sometimes called the City of Magnificent Distances, but it might with greater propriety be termed the City of Magnificent Intentions; for it is only on taking a bird's-eye view of it from the top of the Capitol, that one can at all comprehend the vast designs of its projector, an aspiring Frenchman. Spacious avenues, that begin in nothing, and lead nowhere; streets, mile-long, that only want houses, roads and inhabitants; public buildings that need but a public to be complete; and ornaments of great thoroughfares, which only lack great thoroughfares to ornament – are its leading features. One might fancy the season over, and most of the houses gone out of town for ever with their masters. To the admirers of cities it is a Barmecide Feast: a pleasant field for the imagination to rove in; a monument raised to a deceased project, with not even a legible inscription to record its departed greatness.

Such as it is, it is likely to remain. It was originally chosen for the seat of Government, as a means of averting the conflicting jealousies and interests of the different States; and very probably, too, as being remote from mobs; a consideration not to be slighted, even in America. It has no trade or commerce of its own: having little or no population beyond the President and his establishment; the members of the legislature who reside there during the session; the Government clerks and officers employed in the various departments; the keepers of the hotels and boarding-houses; and the tradesmen who supply their tables. It is very unhealthy. Few people would live in Washington, I take it, who were not obliged to reside there; and the tides of emigration and speculation, those rapid and regardless currents, are little likely to flow at any time towards such dull and sluggish water.

---

33. Richmond

CHAPTER 9

"That travelled creation of the great satirist's brain" is Swift's *Gulliver, who shrank from his fellow men after his sojourn among the noble Houyhnhnms (*Gulliver's Travels, *Book IV).*

The same decay and gloom that overhang the way by which it is approached, hover above the town of Richmond. There are pretty villas and cheerful houses in its streets, and Nature smiles upon the country round; but jostling its handsome residences, like slavery itself going hand in hand with many lofty virtues, are deplorable tenements, fences unrepaired, walls crumbling into ruinous heaps. Hinting gloomily at things below the surface, these, and many other tokens of the same description, force themselves upon the notice, and are remembered with depressing influence, when livelier features are forgotten.

To those who are happily unaccustomed to them, the countenances in the streets and labouring-places, too, are shocking. All men who know that there are laws against instructing slaves, of which the pains and penalties greatly exceed in their amount the fines imposed on those who maim and torture them, must be prepared to find their faces very

"Little Eva Reading the Bible to Uncle Tom," from Uncle Tom's Cabin

low in the scale of intellectual expression. But the darkness – not of skin, but mind – which meets the stranger's eye at every turn; the brutalizing and blotting out of all fairer characters traced by Nature's hand; immeasurably outdo his worst belief. That travelled creation of the great satirist's brain, who fresh from living among horses, peered from a high casement down upon his own kind with trembling horror, was scarcely more repelled and daunted by the sight, than those who look upon some of these faces for the first time must surely be.

I left the last of them behind me in the person of a wretched drudge, who, after running to and fro all day till midnight, and moping in his stealthy winks of sleep upon the stairs betweenwhile, was washing the dark passages at four o'clock in the morning; and went upon my way with a grateful heart that I was not doomed to live where slavery was, and had never had my senses blunted to its wrongs and horrors in a slave-rocked cradle.

34. Pittsburgh

CHAPTER 10

Pages 132–133
*Pittsburgh from
the Soldiers' Mon-
ument*

Pages 134–135
*Cincinnati from
the Carlisle Hotel*

*For details of Dickens' sojourn in this city, see "Dickens in Pitts-
burgh: A Stereoscopic View," by Marilyn P. Hollinshead*, The
Dickensian, *vol. 74 (January 1978), pp. 33–41.*

Pittsburg is like Birmingham in England; at least its townspeople say
so. Setting aside the streets, the shops, the houses, waggons, factories,
public buildings, and population, perhaps it may be. It certainly has a
great quantity of smoke hanging about it, and is famous for its iron-
works. Besides the prison to which I have already referred, this town
contains a pretty arsenal and other institutions. It is very beautifully
situated on the Alleghany River, over which there are two bridges;
and the villas of the wealthier citizens sprinkled about the high
grounds in the neighbourhood, are pretty enough. We lodged at a
most excellent hotel, and were admirably served. As usual it was full
of boarders, was very large, and had a broad colonnade to every story
of the house.

35. Cincinnati

CHAPTER 10

Cincinnati is a beautiful city; cheerful, thriving, and animated. I have
not often seen a place that commends itself so favourably and pleasantly to a stranger at the first glance as this does: with its clean houses
of red and white, its well-paved roads, and foot-ways of bright tile.
Nor does it become less prepossessing on a closer acquaintance. The
streets are broad and airy, the shops extremely good, the private residences remarkable for their elegance and neatness. There is something
of invention and fancy in the varying styles of these latter erections,
which, after the dull company of the steamboat, is perfectly delightful,
as conveying an assurance that there are such qualities still in existence.
The disposition to ornament these pretty villas and render them at-
tractive, leads to the culture of trees and flowers, and the laying out of
well-kept gardens, the sight of which, to those who walk along the
streets, is inexpressibly refreshing and agreeable. I was quite charmed
with the appearance of the town, and its adjoining suburb of Mount

Auburn: from which the city, lying in an amphitheatre of hills, forms a picture of remarkable beauty, and is seen to great advantage.

.   .   .   .

Cincinnati is honourably famous for its free schools, of which it has so many that no person's child among its population, can, by possibility, want the means of education, which are extended, upon an average, to four thousand pupils, annually. I was only present in one of these establishments during the hours of instruction. In the boys' department, which was full of little urchins (varying in their ages, I should say, from six years old to ten or twelve), the master offered to institute an extemporary examination of the pupils in algebra; a proposal, which, as I was by no means confident of my ability to detect mistakes in that science, I declined with some alarm. In the girls' school, reading was proposed; and as I felt tolerably equal to that art, I expressed my willingness to hear a class. Books were distributed accordingly, and some half-dozen girls relieved each other in reading paragraphs from English history. But it seemed to be a dry compilation, infinitely above their powers; and when they had blundered through three or four dreary passages concerning the Treaty of Amiens, and other thrilling topics of the same nature (obviously without comprehending ten words), I expressed myself quite satisfied. It is very possible that they only mounted to this exalted stave in the Ladder of Learning for the astonishment of a visitor; and that at other times they keep upon its lower rounds; but I should have been much better pleased and satisfied if I had heard them exercised in simpler lessons, which they understood.

LANDSCAPES

36. New England

CHAPTER 5

These towns and cities of New England (many of which would be villages in Old England), are as favourable specimens of rural America, as their people are of rural Americans. The well-trimmed lawns and green meadows of home are not there; and the grass, compared with our ornamental plots and pastures, is rank, and rough, and wild: but delicate slopes of land, gently-swelling hills, wooded valleys, and slender streams, abound. Every little colony of houses has its church and school-house peeping from among the white roofs and shady trees; every house is the whitest of the white; every Venetian blind the greenest of the green; every fine day's sky the bluest of the blue. A sharp dry wind and a slight frost had so hardened the roads when we alighted at Worcester, that their furrowed tracks were like ridges of granite. There was the usual aspect of newness on every object, of course. All the buildings looked as if they had been built and painted that morning, and could be taken down on Monday with very little trouble. In the keen evening air, every sharp outline looked a hundred times sharper than ever. The clean cardboard colonnades had no more perspective than a Chinese bridge on a teacup, and appeared equally well calculated for use. The razor-like edges of the detached cottages seemed to cut the very wind as it whistled against them, and to send it smarting on its way with a shriller cry than before. Those slightly-built wooden dwellings behind which the sun was setting with a brilliant lustre, could be so looked through and through, that the idea of any inhabitant being able to hide himself from the public gaze, or to have any secrets from the public eye, was not entertainable for a moment. Even where a blazing fire shone through the uncurtained windows of some distant house, it had the air of being newly lighted, and of lacking warmth; and instead of awakening thoughts of a snug chamber, bright with faces that first saw the light round that same hearth, and ruddy with warm hangings, it came upon one suggestive of the smell of new mortar and damp walls.

*Main Street,
Worcester, Mas-
sachusetts*

*Court Square,
Springfield, Mas-
sachusetts*

37. Virginia: Fredericksburg to Richmond

CHAPTER 9

*"Black and White,"
by Marcus Stone,
from* American
Notes

In this district, as in all others where slavery sits brooding, (I have frequently heard this admitted, even by those who are its warmest advo-
cates:) there is an air of ruin and decay abroad, which is inseparable
from the system. The barns and outhouses are mouldering away; the
sheds are patched and half roofless; the log cabins (built in Virginia
with external chimneys made of clay or wood) are squalid in the last
degree. There is no look of decent comfort anywhere. The miserable
stations by the railway side; the great wild wood-yards, whence the
engine is supplied with fuel; the negro children rolling on the ground
before the cabin doors, with dogs and pigs; the biped beasts of burden
slinking past: gloom and dejection are upon them all.

In the negro car belonging to the train in which we made this journey, were a mother and her children who had just been purchased; the husband and father being left behind with their old owner. The children cried the whole way, and the mother was misery's picture. The champion of Life, Liberty, and the Pursuit of Happiness, who had bought them, rode in the same train; and, every time we stopped, got down to see that they were safe. The black in Sinbad's Travels with one eye in the middle of his forehead which shone like a burning coal, was nature's aristocrat compared with this white gentleman.

---

38. The banks of the Mississippi

CHAPTER 12

Nor was the scenery, as we approached the junction of the Ohio and Mississippi rivers, at all inspiriting in its influence. The trees were stunted in their growth; the banks were low and flat; the settlements and log cabins fewer in number; their inhabitants more wan and wretched than any we had encountered yet. No songs of birds were in the air, no pleasant scents, no moving lights and shadows from swift passing clouds. Hour after hour, the changeless glare of the hot, unwinking sky, shone upon the same monotonous objects. Hour after hour, the river rolled along, as wearily and slowly as the time itself.

At length, upon the morning of the third day, we arrived at a spot so much more desolate than any we had yet beheld, that the forlornest places we had passed, were, in comparison with it, full of interest. At the junction of the two rivers, on ground so flat and low and marshy, that at certain seasons of the year it is inundated to the house-tops, lies a breeding-place of fever, ague, and death; vaunted in England as a mine of Golden Hope, and speculated in, on the faith of monstrous representations, to many people's ruin. A dismal swamp, on which the half-built houses rot away: cleared here and there for the space of a few yards; and teeming, then, with rank unwholesome vegetation, in whose baleful shade the wretched wanderers who are tempted hither, droop, and die, and lay their bones; the hateful Mississippi circling and eddying before it, and turning off upon its southern course a slimy monster hideous to behold; a hotbed of disease, an ugly sepulchre, a grave uncheered by any gleam of promise: a place without one single quality, in earth or air or water, to commend it: such is this dismal Cairo.

But what words shall describe the Mississippi, great father of rivers,

who (praise be to Heaven) has no young children like him! An enormous ditch, sometimes two or three miles wide, running liquid mud,
six miles an hour: its strong and frothy current choked and obstructed
everywhere by huge logs and whole forest trees: now twining themselves together in great rafts, from the interstices of which a sedgy
lazy foam works up, to float upon the water's top; now rolling past
like monstrous bodies, their tangled roots showing like matted hair;
now glancing singly by like giant leeches; and now writhing round
and round in the vortex of some small whirlpool, like wounded snakes.
The banks low, the trees dwarfish, the marshes swarming with frogs,
the wretched cabins few and far apart, their inmates hollow-cheeked
and pale, the weather very hot, mosquitoes penetrating into every
crack and crevice of the boat, mud and slime on everything: nothing
pleasant in its aspect, but the harmless lightning which flickers every
night upon the dark horizon.

*"Cairo. Mouth of
the Ohio," litho-
graph by Arnz &
Co., from Henry
Lewis, Das illus-
trierte Mississippi-
thal (Düsseldorf,
1857)*

39. Niagara

CHAPTER 14

We called at the town of Erie, at eight o'clock that night, and lay there an hour. Between five and six next morning, we arrived at Buffalo, where we breakfasted; and being too near the Great Falls to wait patiently anywhere else, we set off by the train, the same morning at nine o'clock, to Niagara.

It was a miserable day; chilly and raw; a damp mist falling; and the trees in that northern region quite bare and wintry. Whenever the train halted, I listened for the roar; and was constantly straining my eyes in the direction where I knew the Falls must be, from seeing the river rolling on towards them; every moment expecting to behold the spray. Within a few minutes of our stopping, not before, I saw two great white clouds rising up slowly and majestically from the depths of the earth. That was all. At length we alighted: and then for the first time, I heard the mighty rush of water, and felt the ground tremble underneath my feet.

The bank is very steep, and was slippery with rain, and half-melted ice. I hardly know how I got down, but I was soon at the bottom, and climbing, with two English officers who were crossing and had joined me, over some broken rocks, deafened by the noise, half-blinded by the spray, and wet to the skin. We were at the foot of the American Fall. I could see an immense torrent of water tearing headlong down from some great height, but had no idea of shape, or situation, or anything but vague immensity.

When we were seated in the little ferry-boat, and were crossing the swollen river immediately before both cataracts, I began to feel what it was: but I was in a manner stunned, and unable to comprehend the vastness of the scene. It was not until I came on Table Rock, and looked – Great Heaven, on what a fall of bright-green water! – that it came upon me in its full might and majesty.

Then, when I felt how near to my Creator I was standing, the first effect, and the enduring one – instant and lasting – of the tremendous spectacle, was Peace. Peace of Mind, tranquillity, calm recollections of the Dead, great thoughts of Eternal Rest and Happiness; nothing of gloom or terror. Niagara was at once stamped upon my heart, an Image of Beauty; to remain there, changeless and indelible, until its pulses cease to beat, for ever.

Oh, how the strife and trouble of daily life receded from my view, and lessened in the distance, during the ten memorable days we passed on that Enchanted Ground! What voices spoke from out the thundering water; what faces, faded from the earth, looked out upon me from

Under Table Rock in 1835

Pages 144–145
Niagara from the American side

its gleaming depths; what Heavenly promise glistened in those angels' tears, the drops of many hues, that showered around, and twined themselves about the gorgeous arches which the changing rainbows made!

INSTITUTIONS

40. Law courts

CHAPTER 3

To an Englishman, accustomed to the paraphernalia of Westminster
Hall, an American Court of Law, is as odd a sight as, I suppose, an
English Court of Law would be to an American. Except in the Su-
preme Court at Washington (where the judges wear a plain black
robe), there is no such thing as a wig or gown connected with the
administration of justice. The gentlemen of the bar being barristers
and attorneys too (for there is no division of those functions as in
England) are no more removed from their clients than attorneys in
our Court for the Relief of Insolvent Debtors are, from theirs. The
jury are quite at home, and make themselves as comfortable as circumstances will permit. The witness is so little elevated above, or put aloof
from, the crowd in the court, that a stranger entering during a pause
in the proceedings would find it difficult to pick him out from the rest.
And if it chanced to be a criminal trial, his eyes, in nine cases out of
ten, would wander to the dock in search of the prisoner, in vain; for
that gentleman would most likely be lounging among the most distinguished ornaments of the legal profession, whispering suggestions
in his counsel's ear, or making a toothpick out of an old quill with his
penknife.

I could not but notice these differences, when I visited the courts at
Boston. I was much surprised at first, too, to observe that the counsel
who interrogated the witness under examination at the time, did so
sitting. But seeing that he was also occupied in writing down the answers, and remembering that he was alone and had no "junior," I
quickly consoled myself with the reflection that law was not quite so
expensive an article here, as at home; and that the absence of sundry
formalities which we regard as indispensable, had doubtless a very
favourable influence upon the bill of costs.

In every Court, ample and commodious provision is made for the
accommodation of the citizens. This is the case all through America.
In every Public Institution, the right of the people to attend, and to
have an interest in the proceedings, is most fully and distinctly recognised. There are no grim doorkeepers to dole out their tardy civility
by the sixpenny-worth; nor is there, I sincerely believe, any insolence
of office of any kind. Nothing national is exhibited for money; and no
public officer is a showman. We have begun of late years to imitate

Courthouse, Court Square, Boston

this good example. I hope we shall continue to do so; and that in the fullness of time, even deans and chapters may be converted.

. . . .

I am by no means a wholesale admirer of our legal solemnities, many of which impress me as being exceedingly ludicrous. Strange as it may seem too, there is undoubtedly a degree of protection in the wig and gown – a dismissal of individual responsibility in dressing for the part – which encourages that insolent bearing and language, and that gross perversion of the office of a pleader for The Truth, so frequent in our courts of law. Still, I cannot help doubting whether America, in her desire to shake off the absurdities and abuses of the old system, may not have gone too far into the opposite extreme; and whether it is not desirable, especially in the small community of a city like this, where each man knows the other, to surround the administration of justice with some artificial barriers against the "Hail fellow, well met" deportment of everyday life. All the aid it can have in the very high character and ability of the Bench, not only here but elsewhere, it has, and well deserves to have; but it may need something more: not to impress the thoughtful and the well-informed, but the ignorant and heedless; a class which includes some prisoners and many witnesses. These institutions were established, no doubt, upon the principle that those who had so large a share in making the laws, would certainly respect them. But experience has proved this hope to be fallacious; for no men know better than the Judges of America, that on the occasion of any great popular excitement the law is powerless, and cannot, for the time, assert its own supremacy.

41. A lunatic asylum

CHAPTER 6

The asylum Dickens is describing was on Long Island.

The terrible crowd with which these halls and galleries were filled, so shocked me, that I abridged my stay within the shortest limits, and declined to see that portion of the building in which the refractory and violent were under closer restraint. I have no doubt that the gentleman who presided over this establishment at the time I write of, was competent to manage it, and had done all in his power to promote its usefulness: but will it be believed that the miserable strife of Party feeling is carried even into this sad refuge of afflicted and degraded humanity? Will it be believed that the eyes which are to watch over and control the wanderings of minds on which the most dreadful visitation to which our nature is exposed has fallen, must wear the glasses of some wretched side in Politics? Will it be believed that the governor of such a house as this, is appointed, and deposed, and changed perpetually, as Parties fluctuate and vary, and as their despicable weathercocks are blown this way or that? A hundred times in every week, some new most paltry exhibition of that narrow-minded and injurious Party Spirit, which is the Simoom of America, sickening and blighting everything of wholesome life within its reach, was forced upon my notice; but I never turned my back upon it with feelings of such deep disgust and measureless contempt, as when I crossed the threshold of this madhouse.

42. The press

CHAPTERS 14 AND 18

*For Lord Ashburton see the headnote to extract 11 in the first
section of this anthology. The place Dickens is talking about here
is Cleveland.*

I entertained quite a curiosity in reference to this place, from having
seen at Sandusky a specimen of its literature in the shape of a newspaper, which was very strong indeed upon the subject of Lord Ashburton's recent arrival at Washington, to adjust the points in dispute between the United States Government and Great Britain: informing its
readers that as America had "whipped" England in her infancy, and
whipped her again in her youth, so it was clearly necessary that she
must whip her once again in her maturity; and pledging its credit to
all True Americans, that if Mr. Webster did his duty in the approaching negotiations, and sent the English Lord home again in double
quick time, they should, within two years, sing "Yankee Doodle in
Hyde Park, and Hail Columbia in the scarlet courts of Westminster!"
I found it a pretty town, and had the satisfaction of beholding the outside of the office of the journal from which I have just quoted. I did
not enjoy the delight of seeing the wit who indited the paragraph in
question, but I have no doubt he is a prodigious man in his way, and
held in high repute by a select circle.

.   .   .   .

Schools may be erected, East, West, North, and South; pupils be
taught, and masters reared, by scores upon scores of thousands; col-
leges may thrive, churches may be crammed, temperance may be diffused, and advancing knowledge in all other forms walk through the
land with giant strides: but while the newspaper press of America is
in, or near, its present abject state, high moral improvement in that
country is hopeless. Year by year, it must and will go back; year by
year, the tone of public feeling must sink lower down; year by year,
the Congress and the Senate must become of less account before all
decent men; and year by year, the memory of the Great Fathers of
the Revolution must be outraged more and more, in the bad life of
their degenerate child.

Among the herd of journals which are published in the States, there
are some, the reader scarcely need be told, of character and credit.
From personal intercourse with accomplished gentlemen connected
with publications of this class, I have derived both pleasure and profit.
But the name of these is Few, and of the other Legion; and the in-

fluence of the good, is powerless to counteract the moral poison of the bad.

Among the gentry of America; among the well-informed and moderate: in the learned professions; at the bar and on the bench: there is, as there can be, but one opinion, in reference to the vicious character of these infamous journals. It is sometimes contended – I will not say strangely, for it is natural to seek excuses for such a disgrace – that their influence is not so great as a visitor would suppose. I must be pardoned for saying that there is no warrant for this plea, and that every fact and circumstance tends directly to the opposite conclusion.

When any man, of any grade of desert in intellect or character, can climb to any public distinction, no matter what, in America, without first grovelling down upon the earth, and bending the knee before this monster of depravity; when any private excellence is safe from its attacks; when any social confidence is left unbroken by it, or any tie of social decency and honour is held in the least regard; when any man in that free country has freedom of opinion, and presumes to think for himself, and speak for himself, without humble reference to a censorship which, for its rampant ignorance and base dishonesty, he utterly loathes and despises in his heart; when those who most acutely feel its infamy and the reproach it casts upon the nation, and who most denounce it to each other, dare to set their heels upon, and crush it openly, in the sight of all men: then, I will believe that its influence is lessening, and men are returning to their manly senses. But while that Press has its evil eye in every house, and its black hand in every appointment in the state, from a president to a postman; while, with ribald slander for its only stock-in-trade, it is the standard literature of an enormous class, who must find their reading in a newspaper, or they will not read at all; so long must its odium be upon the country's head, and so long must the evil it works, be plainly visible in the Republic.

SOCIAL LIFE AND MANNERS

43. Amusements of the ladies of Boston

CHAPTER 3

"Blue" here means "learned," from the term "bluestocking," applied to feminine aspirants to culture from the mid-eighteenth century.

The tone of society in Boston is one of perfect politeness, courtesy, and good breeding. The ladies are unquestionably very beautiful – in face: but there I am compelled to stop. Their education is much as with us; neither better nor worse. I had heard some very marvellous stories in this respect; but not believing them, was not disappointed. Blue ladies there are, in Boston; but like philosophers of that colour and sex in most other latitudes, they rather desire to be thought superior than to be so. Evangelical ladies there are, likewise, whose attachment to the forms of religion, and horror of theatrical entertainments, are most exemplary. Ladies who have a passion for attending lectures are to be found among all classes and all conditions. In the kind of provincial life which prevails in cities such as this, the Pulpit has great influence. The peculiar province of the Pulpit in New England (always excepting the Unitarian Ministry) would appear to be the denouncement of all innocent and rational amusements. The church, the chapel, and the lecture-room, are the only means of excitement excepted; and to the church, the chapel, and the lecture-room, the ladies resort in crowds.

　Wherever religion is resorted to, as a strong drink, and as an escape from the dull monotonous round of home, those of its ministers who pepper the highest will be the surest to please. They who strew the Eternal Path with the greatest amount of brimstone, and who most ruthlessly tread down the flowers and leaves that grow by the wayside, will be voted the most righteous; and they who enlarge with the greatest pertinacity on the difficulty of getting into heaven, will be considered by all true believers certain of going there: though it would be hard to say by what process of reasoning this conclusion is arrived at. It is so at home, and it is so abroad. With regard to the other means of excitement, the Lecture, it has at least the merit of being always new. One lecture treads so quickly on the heels of another, that none are remembered; and the course of this month may be safely repeated next, with its charm of novelty unbroken, and its interest unabated.

*The Athenaeum,
Beacon Street,
Boston*

*Park Street church
about 1850, Boston*

44. Communal meals on a canal boat

CHAPTER II

We are to be on board "The Messenger" three days: arriving at Cincinnati (barring accidents) on Monday morning. There are three meals a day. Breakfast at seven, dinner at half-past twelve, supper about six. At each, there are a great many small dishes and plates upon the table, with very little in them; so that although there is every appearance of a mighty "spread," there is seldom really more than a joint: except for those who fancy slices of beet-root, shreds of dried beef, complicated entanglements of yellow pickle; maize, Indian corn, apple-sauce, and pumpkin.

Some people fancy all these little dainties together (and sweet preserves beside), by way of relish to their roast pig. They are generally those dyspeptic ladies and gentlemen who eat unheard-of quantities of hot corn bread (almost as good for the digestion as a kneaded pincushion), for breakfast, and for supper. Those who do not observe this custom, and who help themselves several times instead, usually suck their knives and forks meditatively, until they have decided what to take next: then pull them out of their mouths: put them in the dish; help themselves; and fall to work again. At dinner, there is nothing to drink upon the table, but great jugs of cold water. Nobody says

The Mississippi steamboat, The Messenger

anything, at any meal, to anybody. All the passengers are very dismal, and seem to have tremendous secrets weighing on their minds. There is no conversation, no laughter, no cheerfulness, no sociality, except in spitting; and that is done in silent fellowship round the stove, when the meal is over. Every man sits down, dull and languid; swallows his fare as if breakfasts, dinners, and suppers, were necessities of nature never to be coupled with recreation or enjoyment; and having bolted his food in a gloomy silence, bolts himself, in the same state. But for these animal observances, you might suppose the whole male portion of the company to be the melancholy ghosts of departed book-keepers, who had fallen dead at the desk: such is their weary air of business and calculation. Undertakers on duty would be sprightly beside them; and a collation of funeral baked-meats, in comparison with these meals, would be a sparkling festivity.

---

45. A roadside conversation

CHAPTER 14

Whenever the coach stops, and you can hear the voices of the inside passengers; or whenever any bystander addresses them, or any one among them; or they address each other; you will hear one phrase repeated over and over and over again to the most extraordinary extent. It is an ordinary and unpromising phrase enough, being neither more nor less than "Yes, Sir"; but it is adapted to every variety of circumstance, and fills up every pause in the conversation. Thus: –

The time is one o'clock at noon. The scene, a place where we are to stay and dine, on this journey. The coach drives up to the door of an inn. The day is warm, and there are several idlers lingering about the tavern, and waiting for the public dinner. Among them, is a stout gentleman in a brown hat, swinging himself to and fro in a rocking-chair on the pavement.

As the coach stops, a gentleman in a straw hat looks out of the window:

STRAW HAT. (To the stout gentleman in the rocking-chair.) I reckon that's Judge Jefferson, an't it?

BROWN HAT. (Still swinging; speaking very slowly; and without any emotion whatever.) Yes, Sir.

STRAW HAT. Warm weather, Judge.

BROWN HAT. Yes, Sir.

STRAW HAT. There was a snap of cold, last week.

"*As the coach
stops, a gentleman
in a straw hat looks
out of the win-
dow,*" *from* Ameri-
can Notes

BROWN HAT. Yes, Sir.

STRAW HAT. Yes, Sir.

A pause. They look at each other, very seriously.

STRAW HAT. I calculate you'll have got through that case of the corporation, Judge, by this time, now?

BROWN HAT. Yes, Sir.

STRAW HAT. How did the verdict go, Sir?

BROWN HAT. For the defendant, Sir.

STRAW HAT. (Interrogatively.) Yes, Sir?

BROWN HAT. (Affirmatively.) Yes, Sir.

BOTH. (Musingly, as each gazes down the street.) Yes, Sir.

Another pause. They look at each other again, still more seriously
than before.

BROWN HAT. This coach is rather behind its time to-day, I guess.

STRAW HAT. (Doubtingly.) Yes, Sir.

BROWN HAT. (Looking at his watch.) Yes, Sir; nigh upon two hours.

STRAW HAT. (Raising his eyebrows in very great surprise.) Yes, Sir!

BROWN HAT. (Decisively, as he puts up his watch.) Yes, Sir.

ALL THE OTHER INSIDE PASSENGERS. (Among themselves.) Yes, Sir.

COACHMAN. (In a very surly tone.) No it an't.

STRAW HAT. (To the coachman.) Well, I don't know, Sir. We were a pretty tall time coming that last fifteen mile. That's a fact.

The coachman making no reply, and plainly declining to enter into any controversy on a subject so far removed from his sympathies and feelings, another passenger says, "Yes, Sir"; and the gentleman in the straw hat in acknowledgment of his courtesy, says "Yes, Sir," to him, in return. The straw hat then inquires of the brown hat, whether that coach in which he (the straw hat) then sits, is not a new one? To which the brown hat makes answer, "Yes, Sir."

STRAW HAT. I thought so. Pretty loud smell of varnish Sir?

BROWN HAT. Yes, Sir.

ALL THE OTHER INSIDE PASSENGERS. Yes, Sir.

BROWN HAT. (To the company in general.) Yes, Sir.

The conversational powers of the company having been by this time pretty heavily taxed, the straw hat opens the door and gets out; and all the rest alight also.

CHARACTERS

46. Factory girls

CHAPTER 4

Dickens is describing the celebrated textile mills in Lowell, Massachusetts. "Nowhere in America," comment the editors of the Penguin English Library Edition of American Notes, *"were factory workers treated so paternally as here."*

These girls, as I have said, were all well dressed: and that phrase necessarily includes extreme cleanliness. They had serviceable bonnets, good warm cloaks, and shawls; and were not above clogs and pattens. Moreover, there were places in the mill in which they could deposit these things without injury; and there were conveniences for washing. They were healthy in appearance, many of them remarkably so, and had the manners and deportment of young women: not of degraded brutes of burden. If I had seen in one of those mills (but I did not, though I looked for something of this kind with a sharp eye), the most lisping, mincing, affected, and ridiculous young creature that my imagination could suggest, I should have thought of the careless, moping, slatternly, degraded, dull reverse (I *have* seen that), and should have been still well pleased to look upon her.

The rooms in which they worked, were as well ordered as themselves. In the windows of some, there were green plants, which were trained to shade the glass; in all, there was as much fresh air, cleanliness, and comfort, as the nature of the occupation would possibly admit of. Out of so large a number of females, many of whom were only then just verging upon womanhood, it may be reasonably supposed that some were delicate and fragile in appearance: no doubt there were. But I solemnly declare, that from all the crowd I saw in the different factories that day, I cannot recall or separate one young face that gave me a painful impression; nor one young girl whom, assuming it to be matter of necessity that she should gain her daily bread by the labour of her hands, I would have removed from those works if I had had the power.

. . . .

I am now going to state three facts, which will startle a large class of readers on this side of the Atlantic, very much.

Firstly, there is a joint-stock piano in a great many of the boarding-

Merrimack mills and boarding-houses, Lowell, from W. Glyde Wilkins' Charles Dickens in America

houses. Secondly, nearly all these young ladies subscribe to circulating libraries. Thirdly, they have got up among themselves a periodical called THE LOWELL OFFERING, "A repository of original articles, written exclusively by females actively employed in the mills," – which is duly printed, published, and sold; and whereof I brought away from Lowell four hundred good solid pages, which I have read from beginning to end.

The large class of readers, startled by these facts, will exclaim, with one voice, "How very preposterous!" On my deferentially inquiring why, they will answer, "These things are above their station." In reply to that objection, I would beg to ask what their station is.

It is their station to work. And they *do* work. They labour in these mills, upon an average, twelve hours a day, which is unquestionably work, and pretty tight work too. Perhaps it is above their station to indulge in such amusements, on any terms. Are we quite sure that we in England have not formed our ideas of the "station" of working people, from accustoming ourselves to the contemplation of that class as they are, and not as they might be? I think that if we examine our own feelings, we shall find the pianos, and the circulating libraries, and even the Lowell Offering, startle us by their novelty, and not by their bearing upon any abstract question of right or wrong.

. . . .

Of the merits of the Lowell Offering as a literary production, I will only observe, putting entirely out of sight the fact of the articles having been written by these girls after the arduous labours of the day, that it will compare advantageously with a great many English Annuals. It is pleasant to find that many of its Tales are of the Mills and of those who work in them; that they inculcate habits of self-denial

THE VOICE OF PEACE.

I heard a voice come from a leafy bower,
I stood, enchanted by its magic power;
   'Twas in the birds' sweet warbling, soft and clear;
'Twas in the murmuring of the summer breeze;
'Twas in the rustling foliage of the trees;
   In those sweet sounds it whispered, "Peace is here!"

I heard a voice come from a cottage hearth,
Where sate a peasant group, in happy mirth,
   Singing their rustic song, devoid of fear.
And, as I slowly trod my thoughtful way,
It rose, and with the cotter's evening lay
   It loudly, gladly warbled, "Peace is here!"

I heard a voice come from the churchyard's gloom;
From the dread calmness of the silent tomb;
   It wandered through the foliage dry and sere;
'Twas where the willow's weeping branches wave
Above the lonely stillness of the grave;
   And mournfully it echoed, "Peace is here!"

and contentment, and teach good doctrines of enlarged benevolence. A strong feeling for the beauties of nature, as displayed in the solitudes the writers have left at home, breathes through its pages like wholesome village air; and though a circulating library is a favourable school for the study of such topics, it has very scant allusion to fine clothes, fine marriages, fine houses, or fine life. Some persons might object to the papers being signed occasionally with rather fine names, but this is an American fashion. One of the provinces of the state legislature of Massachusetts is to alter ugly names into pretty ones, as the children improve upon the tastes of their parents. These changes costing little or nothing, scores of Mary Annes are solemnly converted into Bevelinas every session.

47. Broadway loungers (porcine)

CHAPTER 6

Gil Blas is the hero of one of the favourite books of Dickens' childhood, Le Sage's picaresque novel (1715) named after the character.

Once more in Broadway! Here are the same ladies in bright colours, walking to and fro, in pairs and singly; yonder the very same light blue parasol which passed and repassed the hotel-window twenty times while we were sitting there. We are going to cross here. Take care of the pigs. Two portly sows are trotting up behind this carriage, and a select party of half-a-dozen gentlemen hogs have just now turned the corner.

Here is a solitary swine lounging homeward by himself. He has only one ear; having parted with the other to vagrant-dogs in the course of his city rambles. But he gets on very well without it; and leads a roving, gentlemanly, vagabond kind of life, somewhat answering to that of our club-men at home. He leaves his lodgings every morning at a certain hour, throws himself upon the town, gets through his day in some manner quite satisfactory to himself, and regularly appears at the door of his own house again at night, like the mysterious master of Gil Blas. He is a free-and-easy, careless, indifferent kind of pig, having a very large acquaintance among other pigs of the same character, whom he rather knows by sight than conversation, as he seldom troubles himself to stop and exchange civilities, but goes grunting down the kennel, turning up the news and small-talk of the city in the shape of cabbage-stalks and offal, and bearing no tails but his own: which is a very short one, for his old enemies, the dogs, have been at that too, and have left him hardly enough to swear by. He is in every respect a republican pig, going wherever he pleases, and mingling with the best society, on an equal, if not superior footing, for every one makes way when he appears, and the haughtiest give him the wall, if he prefer it. He is a great philosopher, and seldom moved unless by the dogs before mentioned. Sometimes, indeed, you may see his small eye twinkling on a slaughtered friend, whose carcase garnishes a butcher's door-post, but he grunts out "Such is life: all flesh is pork!" buries his nose in the mire again, and waddles down the gutter: comforting himself with the reflection that there is one snout the less to anticipate stray cabbage-stalks, at any rate.

---

48. Congressmen

CHAPTER 8

Did I see in this public body an assemblage of men, bound together in the sacred names of Liberty, and Freedom, and so asserting the chaste dignity of those twin goddesses, in all their discussions, as to exalt at once the Eternal Principles to which their names are given, and their own character and the character of their countrymen, in the admiring eyes of the whole world?

.   .   .   .

Broadway

I saw in them, the wheels that move the meanest perversion of virtuous Political Machinery that the worst tools ever wrought. Despicable trickery at elections; under-handed tamperings with public officers; cowardly attacks upon opponents, with scurrilous newspapers for shields, and hired pens for daggers; shameful trucklings to mercenary knaves, whose claim to be considered, is, that every day and week they sow new crops of ruin with their venal types, which are the dragon's teeth of yore, in everything but sharpness; aidings and abettings of every bad inclination in the popular mind, and artful suppressions of all its good influences: such things as these, and in a word, Dishonest Faction in its most depraved and most unblushing form, stared out from every corner of the crowded hall.

Torch light procession in New York, 1844

Did I see among them, the intelligence and refinement: the true, honest, patriotic heart of America? Here and there, were drops of its blood and life, but they scarcely coloured the stream of desperate adventurers which sets that way for profit and for pay. It is the game of these men, and of their profligate organs, to make the strife of politics so fierce and brutal, and so destructive of all self-respect in worthy men, that sensitive and delicate-minded persons shall be kept aloof, and they, and such as they, be left to battle out their selfish views unchecked. And thus this lowest of all scrambling fights goes on, and they who in other countries would, from their intelligence and station, most aspire to make the laws, do here recoil the farthest from that degradation.

That there are, among the representatives of the people in both Houses, and among all parties, some men of high character and great abilities, I need not say. The foremost among those politicians who are known in Europe, have been already described, and I see no reason to depart from the rule I have laid down for my guidance, of abstaining from all mention of individuals. It will be sufficient to add, that to the most favourable accounts that have been written of them, I more than fully and most heartily subscribe; and that personal intercourse and free communication have bred within me, not the result predicted in the very doubtful proverb, but increased admiration and respect. They are striking men to look at, hard to deceive, prompt to act, lions in energy, Crichtons in varied accomplishments, Indians in fire of eye and gesture, Americans in strong and generous impulse; and they as well represent the honour and wisdom of their country at home, as the distinguished gentleman who is now its Minister at the British Court sustains its highest character abroad.

49. A Mississippi man

CHAPTER 10

A "Johnny Cake" is made of maize meal toasted or baked in a pan – used as a slang term for New Englanders.

There are two canal lines of passage-boats; one is called The Express, and one (a cheaper one) The Pioneer. The Pioneer gets first to the mountain, and waits for the Express people to come up; both sets of passengers being conveyed across it at the same time. We were the Express company; but when we had crossed the mountain, and had come to the second boat, the proprietors took it into their heads to draft all the Pioneers into it likewise, so that we were five-and-forty at least, and the accession of passengers was not at all of that kind which improved the prospect of sleeping at night. Our people grumbled at this, as people do in such cases; but suffered the boat to be towed off with the whole freight aboard nevertheless; and away we went down the canal. At home, I should have protested lustily, but being a foreigner here, I held my peace. Not so this passenger. He cleft a path among the people on deck (we were nearly all on deck), and without addressing anybody whomsoever, soliloquised as follows:

"This may suit *you*, this may, but it don't suit *me*. This may be all very well with Down Easters, and men of Boston raising, but it won't suit my figure nohow; and no two ways about *that*; and so I tell you. Now! I'm from the brown forests of the Mississippi, *I* am, and when the sun shines on me, it does shine – a little. It don't glimmer where *I* live, the sun don't. No. I'm a brown forester, I am. I an't a Johnny Cake. There are no smooth skins where I live. We're rough men there. Rather. If Down Easters and men of Boston raising like this, I'm glad of it, but I'm none of that raising nor of that breed. No. This company wants a little fixing, *it* does. I'm the wrong sort of man for 'em, *I* am. They won't like me, *they* won't. This is piling of it up, a little too mŏuntăinous, this is." At the end of every one of these short sentences he turned upon his heel, and walked the other way; checking himself abruptly when he had finished another short sentence, and turning back again.

It is impossible for me to say what terrific meaning was hidden in the words of this brown forester, but I know that the other passengers looked on in a sort of admiring horror, and that presently the boat was put back to the wharf, and as many of the Pioneers as could be coaxed or bullied into going away, were got rid of.

When we started again, some of the boldest spirits on board, made bold to say to the obvious occasion of this improvement in our prospects, "Much obliged to you, Sir"; whereunto the brown forester (waving his hand, and still walking up and down as before), replied, "No you an't. You're none o' my raising. You may act for yourselves, *you* may. I have pinted out the way. Down Easters and Johnny Cakes can follow if they please. I an't a Johnny Cake, *I* an't. I am from the brown forests of the Mississippi, *I* am" – and so on, as before. He was unanimously voted one of the tables for his bed at night – there is a great contest for the tables – in consideration for his public services: and he had the warmest corner by the stove throughout the rest of the journey. But I never could find out that he did anything except sit there; nor did I hear him speak again until, in the midst of the bustle and turmoil of getting the luggage ashore in the dark at Pittsburg, I stumbled over him as he sat smoking a cigar on the cabin steps, and heard him muttering to himself, with short laugh of defiance, "I an't a Johnny Cake, *I* an't. I'm from the brown forests of the Mississippi, *I* am, damme!" I am inclined to argue from this, that he had never left off saying so; but I could not make an affidavit of that part of the story, if required to do so by my Queen and Country.

---

50. An Indian chief

CHAPTER 12

For "Catlin's gallery" see the headnote to extract 23, above.

There chanced to be on board this boat, in addition to the usual dreary crowd of passengers, one Pitchlynn, a chief of the Choctaw tribe of Indians, who *sent in his card* to me, and with whom I had the pleasure of a long conversation.

He spoke English perfectly well, though he had not begun to learn the language, he told me, until he was a young man grown. He had read many books; and Scott's poetry appeared to have left a strong impression on his mind: especially the opening of the Lady of the Lake, and the great battle scene in Marmion, in which, no doubt from the congeniality of the subjects to his own pursuits and tastes, he had great interest and delight. He appeared to understand correctly all he had read; and whatever fiction had enlisted his sympathy in its belief, had done so keenly and earnestly. I might almost say fiercely. He was dressed in our ordinary every-day costume, which hung about his fine figure loosely, and with indifferent grace. On my telling him that I regretted not to see him in his own attire, he threw up his right arm,

for a moment, as though he were brandishing some heavy weapon, and answered, as he let it fall again, that his race were losing many things besides their dress, and would soon be seen upon the earth no more: but he wore it at home, he added proudly.

He told me that he had been away from his home, west of the Mississippi, seventeen months: and was now returning. He had been chiefly at Washington on some negotiations pending between his Tribe and the Government: which were not settled yet (he said in a melancholy way), and he feared never would be: for what could a few poor Indians do, against such well-skilled men of business as the whites? He had no love for Washington; tired of towns and cities very soon; and longed for the Forest and the Prairie.

I asked him what he thought of Congress? He answered, with a smile, that it wanted dignity, in an Indian's eyes.

He would very much like, he said, to see England before he died; and spoke with much interest about the great things to be seen there. When I told him of that chamber in the British Museum wherein are preserved household memorials of a race that ceased to be thousands of years ago, he was very attentive, and it was not hard to see that he had a reference in his mind to the gradual fading away of his own people.

This led us to speak of Mr. Catlin's gallery, which he praised highly: observing that his own portrait was among the collection, and that all the likenesses were "elegant." Mr. Cooper, he said, had painted the Red Man well; and so would I, he knew, if I would go home with him and hunt buffaloes, which he was quite anxious I should do. When I told him that supposing I went, I should not be very likely to damage the buffaloes much, he took it as a great joke and laughed heartily.

He was a remarkably handsome man; some years past forty, I should judge; with long black hair, an aquiline nose, broad cheek-bones, a sunburnt complexion, and a very bright, keen, dark, and piercing eye. There were but twenty thousand of the Choctaws left, he said, and their number was decreasing every day. A few of his brother chiefs had been obliged to become civilised, and to make themselves acquainted with what the whites knew, for it was their only chance of existence. But they were not many; and the rest were as they always had been. He dwelt on this: and said several times that unless they tried to assimilate themselves to their conquerors, they must be swept away before the strides of civilised society.

Pitchlynn, the Choctaw chief. According to Catlin, "the name of this man is Ha-tchoo-tuck-nee *(the snapping turtle . . .), familiarly called by the whites 'Peter Pinchlin'"*

51. A midwestern couple

CHAPTER 14

The house was kept by a characteristic old couple, with whom we had a long talk, and who were perhaps a very good sample of that kind of people in the West.

The landlord was a dry, tough, hard-faced old fellow (not so very old either, for he was but just turned sixty, I should think), who had been out with the militia in the last war with England, and had seen all kinds of service, – except a battle; and he had been very near seeing that, he added: very near. He had all his life been restless and loco-motive, with an irresistible desire for change; and was still the son of his old self: for if he had nothing to keep him at home, he said (slightly jerking his hat and his thumb towards the window of the room in which the old lady sat, as we stood talking in front of the house), he would clean up his musket, and be off to Texas to-morrow morning. He was one of the very many descendants of Cain proper to this continent, who seem destined from their birth to serve as pioneers in the great human army: who gladly go on from year to year extending its outposts, and leaving home after home behind them; and die at last, utterly regardless of their graves being left thousands of miles behind, by the wandering generation who succeed.

His wife was a domesticated kind-hearted old soul, who had come with him, "from the queen city of the world," which, it seemed, was Philadelphia; but had no love for this Western country, and indeed had little reason to bear it any; having seen her children, one by one, die here of fever, in the full prime and beauty of their youth. Her heart was sore, she said, to think of them; and to talk on this theme, even to strangers, in that blighted place, so far from her old home, eased it somewhat, and became a melancholy pleasure.

---

52. The Shakers

CHAPTER 16

The house is very pleasantly situated, however, and we had a good breakfast. That done, we went to visit our place of destination, which was some two miles off, and the way to which was soon indicated by a finger-post, whereon was painted, "To the Shaker Village."

As we rode along, we passed a party of Shakers, who were at work upon the road; who wore the broadest of all broad-brimmed hats; and were in all visible respects such very wooden men, that I felt about as much sympathy for them, and as much interest in them, as if they had been so many figure-heads of ships. Presently we came to the beginning of the village, and alighting at the door of a house where the Shaker manufactures are sold, and which is the headquarters of the elders, requested permission to see the Shaker worship.

Pending the conveyance of this request to some person in authority, we walked into a grim room, where several grim hats were hanging on grim pegs, and the time was grimly told by a grim clock which uttered every tick with a kind of struggle, as if it broke the grim silence reluctantly, and under protest. Ranged against the wall were six or eight stiff high-backed chairs, and they partook so strongly of the general grimness that one would much rather have sat on the floor than incurred the smallest obligation to any of them.

Presently, there stalked into this apartment, a grim old Shaker, with eyes as hard, and dull, and cold, as the great round metal buttons on his coat and waistcoat; a sort of calm goblin. Being informed of our desire, he produced a newspaper wherein the body of elders, whereof he was a member, had advertised but a few days before, that in consequence of certain unseemly interruptions which their worship had received from strangers, their chapel was closed to the public for the space of one year.

As nothing was to be urged in opposition to this reasonable arrangement, we requested leave to make some trifling purchases of Shaker goods; which was grimly conceded. We accordingly repaired to a store in the same house and on the opposite side of the passage, where the stock was presided over by something alive in a russet case, which the elder said was a woman; and which I suppose *was* a woman, though I should not have suspected it.

On the opposite side of the road was their place of worship: a cool, clean edifice of wood, with large windows and green blinds: like a spacious summer-house. As there was no getting into this place, and nothing was to be done but walk up and down, and look at it and the other buildings in the village (which were chiefly of wood, painted a dark red like English barns, and composed of many stories like English factories), I have nothing to communicate to the reader, beyond the scanty results I gleaned the while our purchases were making.

These people are called Shakers from their peculiar form of adoration, which consists of a dance, performed by the men and women of all ages, who arrange themselves for that purpose in opposite parties: the men first divesting themselves of their hats and coats, which they gravely hang against the wall before they begin; and tying a ribbon round their shirt-sleeves, as though they were going to be bled. They

The sacred dance of the Shakers

accompany themselves with a droning, humming noise, and dance until they are quite exhausted, alternately advancing and retiring in a preposterous sort of trot. The effect is said to be unspeakably absurd: and if I may judge from a print of this ceremony which I have in my possession; and which I am informed by those who have visited the chapel is perfectly accurate; it must be infinitely grotesque.

They are governed by a woman, and her rule is understood to be absolute, though she has the assistance of a council of elders. She lives, it is said, in strict seclusion, in certain rooms above the chapel, and is never shown to profane eyes. If she at all resemble the lady who presided over the store, it is a great charity to keep her as close as possible, and I cannot too strongly express my perfect concurrence in this benevolent proceeding.

All the possessions and revenues of the settlement are thrown into a common stock, which is managed by the elders. As they have made converts among people who were well to do in the world, and are frugal and thrifty, it is understood that this fund prospers: the more especially as they have made large purchases of land. Nor is this at Lebanon the only Shaker settlement: there are, I think, at least, three others.

They are good farmers, and all their produce is eagerly purchased and highly esteemed. "Shaker seeds," "Shaker herbs," and "Shaker distilled waters," are commonly announced for sale in the shops of towns and cities. They are good breeders of cattle, and are kind and merciful to the brute creation. Consequently, Shaker beasts seldom fail to find a ready market.

They eat and drink together, after the Spartan model, at a great public table. There is no union of the sexes, and every Shaker, male and female, is devoted to a life of celibacy. Rumour has been busy upon this theme, but here again I must refer to the lady of the store, and say, that if many of the sister Shakers resemble her, I treat all such slander as bearing on its face the strongest marks of wild improbability. But that they take as proselytes, persons so young that they cannot know their own minds, and cannot possess much strength of resolution in this or any other respect, I can assert from my own observation of the extreme juvenility of certain youthful Shakers whom I saw at work among the party on the road.

They are said to be good drivers of bargains, but to be honest and just in their transactions, and even in horse-dealing to resist those thievish tendencies which would seem, for some undiscovered reason, to be almost inseparable from that branch of traffic. In all matters they hold their own course quietly, live in their gloomy silent commonwealth, and show little desire to interfere with other people.

---

53. The "artist in boots"

CHAPTER 18

The Republican Institutions of America undoubtedly lead the people to assert their self-respect and their equality; but a traveller is bound to bear those Institutions in his mind, and not hastily to resent the near approach of a class of strangers, who, at home, would keep aloof. This characteristic, when it was tinctured with no foolish pride, and stopped short of no honest service, never offended me; and I very seldom, if ever, experienced its rude or unbecoming display. Once or twice it was comically developed, as in the following case; but this was an amusing incident, and not the rule, or near it.

I wanted a pair of boots at a certain town, for I had none to travel in, but those with the memorable cork soles, which were much too hot for the fiery decks of a steamboat. I therefore sent a message to an artist in boots, importing, with my compliments, that I should be hap-

py to see him, if he would do me the polite favour to call. He very kindly returned for answer, that he would "look round" at six o'clock that evening.

I was lying on the sofa, with a book and a wine-glass, at about that time, when the door opened, and a gentleman in a stiff cravat, within a year or two on either side of thirty, entered, in his hat and gloves; walked up to the looking-glass; arranged his hair; took off his gloves; slowly produced a measure from the uttermost depths of his coat-pocket; and requested me, in a languid tone, to "unfix" my straps. I complied, but looked with some curiosity at his hat, which was still upon his head. It might have been that, or it might have been the heat – but he took it off. Then, he sat himself down on a chair opposite to me; rested an arm on each knee; and, leaning forward very much, took from the ground, by a great effort, the specimen of metropolitan workmanship which I had just pulled off: whistling, pleasantly, as he did so. He turned it over and over; surveyed it with a contempt no language can express; and inquired if I wished him to fix me a boot like *that*? I courteously replied, that provided the boots were large enough, I would leave the rest to him; that if convenient and practicable, I should not object to their bearing some resemblance to the model then before him; but that I would be entirely guided by, and would beg to leave the whole subject to, his judgment and discretion. "You an't partickler, about this scoop in the heel, I suppose then?" says he: "we don't foller that, here." I repeated my last observation. He looked at himself in the glass again; went closer to it to dash a grain or two of dust out of the corner of his eye; and settled his cravat. All this time, my leg and foot were in the air. "Nearly ready, Sir?" I inquired. "Well, pretty nigh," he said; "keep steady." I kept as steady as I could, both in foot and face; and having by this time got the dust out, and found his pencil-case, he measured me, and made the necessary notes. When he had finished, he fell into his old attitude, and taking up the boot again, mused for some time. "And this," he said, at last, "is an English boot, is it? This is a London boot, eh?" "That Sir," I replied, "is a London boot." He mused over it again, after the manner of Hamlet with Yorick's skull; nodded his head, as who should say, "I pity the Institutions that led to the production of this boot"; rose; put up his pencil, notes, and paper – glancing at himself in the glass, all the time – put on his hat; drew on his gloves very slowly; and finally walked out. When he had been gone about a minute, the door reopened, and his hat and head reappeared. He looked round the room, and at the boot again, which was still lying on the floor; appeared thoughtful for a minute; and then said "Well, good arternoon." "Good afternoon, Sir," said I: and that was the end of the interview.

NATIONAL CHARACTERISTICS

54. "An innumerable brood of evils"

CHAPTER 18

It is an essential part of every national character to pique itself mightily upon its faults, and to deduce tokens of its virtue or its wisdom from their very exaggeration. One great blemish in the popular mind of America, and the prolific parent of an innumerable brood of evils, is Universal Distrust. Yet the American citizen plumes himself upon this spirit, even when he is sufficiently dispassionate to perceive the ruin it works; and will often adduce it, in spite of his own reason, as an instance of the great sagacity and acuteness of the people, and their superior shrewdness and independence.

"You carry," says the stranger, "this jealousy and distrust into every transaction of public life. By repelling worthy men from your legislative assemblies, it has bred up a class of candidates for the suffrage, who, in their every act, disgrace your Institutions and your people's choice. It has rendered you so fickle, and so given to change, that your inconstancy has passed into a proverb; for you no sooner set up an idol firmly, than you are sure to pull it down and dash it into fragments: and this, because directly you reward a benefactor, or a public servant, you distrust him, merely because he *is* rewarded; and immediately apply yourselves to find out, either that you have been too bountiful in your acknowledgments, or he remiss in his deserts. Any man who attains a high place among you, from the President downwards, may date his downfall from that moment; for any printed lie that any notorious villain pens, although it militate directly against the character and conduct of a life, appeals at once to your distrust, and is believed. You will strain at a gnat in the way of trustfulness and confidence, however fairly won and well deserved; but you will swallow a whole caravan of camels, if they be laden with unworthy doubts and mean suspicions. Is this well, think you, or likely to elevate the character of the governors or the governed, among you?"

The answer is invariably the same: "There's freedom of opinion here, you know. Every man thinks for himself, and we are not to be easily overreached. That's how our people come to be suspicious."

Another prominent feature is the love of "smart" dealing: which gilds over many a swindle and gross breach of trust; many a defalcation, public and private; and enables many a knave to hold his head up with the best, who well deserves a halter; though it has not been without its retributive operation, for this smartness has done more in a few years to impair the public credit, and to cripple the public resources, than dull honesty, however rash, could have effected in a century. The merits of a broken speculation, or a bankruptcy, or of a successful scoundrel, are not gauged by its or his observance of the golden rule, "Do as you would be done by," but are considered with reference to their smartness. I recollect, on both occasions of our passing that ill-fated Cairo on the Mississippi, remarking on the bad effects such gross deceits must have when they exploded, in generating a want of confidence abroad, and discouraging foreign investment: but I was given to understand that this was a very smart scheme by which a deal of money had been made; and that its smartest feature was, that they forgot these things abroad, in a very short time, and speculated again, as freely as ever. The following dialogue I have held a hundred times: "Is it not a very disgraceful circumstance that such a man as So-and-so should be acquiring a large property by the most infamous and odious means, and notwithstanding all the crimes of which he has been guilty, should be tolerated and abetted by your Citizens? He is a public nuisance, is he not?" "Yes, Sir." "A convicted liar?" "Yes, Sir." "He has been kicked, and cuffed, and caned?" "Yes, Sir." "And he is utterly dishonourable, debased, and profligate?" "Yes, Sir." "In the name of wonder, then, what is his merit?" "Well, Sir, he is a smart man."

III. *Martin Chuzzlewit*

55. The New York press

CHAPTER 16

The term "loco-foco" is not a Dickensian extravagance. In "American Party Names," published in Dickens' journal Household Words *on 9 August 1856, the writer explains that, earlier in the century, at a Democratic convention in New York, "the friends of a certain candidate for that party's support, finding themselves likely to be out-*

Printing House Square, New York, 1866

voted, attempted to break up the meeting by putting out the lights:
the friends of the opposing candidate, however, remained; and one of
them, having in his pocket some matches of the sort then called
loco-foco, re-lighted the lamps, and the meeting was re-organised.
Hence the term Loco-foco was first applied to one of these temporary
local divisions: afterwards it came to have a wider application."

Some trifling excitement prevailed upon the very brink and margin of
the land of liberty; for an alderman had been elected the day before;

and Party Feeling naturally running rather high on such an exciting occasion, the friends of the disappointed candidate had found it necessary to assert the great principles of Purity of Election and Freedom of Opinion by breaking a few legs and arms, and furthermore pursuing one obnoxious gentleman through the streets with the design of slitting his nose. These good-humoured little outbursts of the popular fancy were not in themselves sufficiently remarkable to create any great stir, after the lapse of a whole night; but they found fresh life and notoriety in the breath of the newsboys, who not only proclaimed them with shrill yells in all the highways and by-ways of the town, upon the wharves and among the shipping, but on the deck and down in the cabins of the steamboat; which, before she touched the shore, was boarded and overrun by a legion of those young citizens.

'Here's this morning's New York Sewer!' cried one. 'Here's this morning's New York Stabber! Here's the New York Family Spy! Here's the New York Private Listener! Here's the New York Peeper! Here's the New York Plunderer! Here's the New York Keyhole Reporter! Here's the New York Rowdy Journal! Here's all the New York papers! Here's full particulars of the patriotic loco-foco movement yesterday, in which the whigs was so chawed up; and the last Alabama gouging case; and the interesting Arkansas dooel with Bowie knives; and all the Political, Commercial, and Fashionable News. Here they are! Here they are! Here's the papers, here's the papers!'

'Here's the Sewer!' cried another. 'Here's the New York Sewer! Here's some of the twelfth thousand of today's Sewer, with the best accounts of the markets, and all the shipping news, and four whole columns of country correspondence, and a full account of the Ball at Mrs. White's last night, where all the beauty and fashion of New York was assembled; with the Sewer's own particulars of the private lives of all the ladies that was there! Here's the Sewer! Here's some of the twelfth thousand of the New York Sewer! Here's the Sewer's exposure of the Wall Street Gang, and the Sewer's exposure of the Washington gang, and the Sewer's exclusive account of a flagrant act of dishonesty committed by the Secretary of State when he was eight years old; now communicated, at a great expense, by his own nurse. Here's the Sewer! Here's the New York Sewer, in its twelfth thousand, with a whole column of New Yorkers to be shown up, and all their names printed! Here's the Sewer's article upon the Judge that tried him, day afore yesterday, for libel, and the Sewer's tribute to the independent Jury that didn't convict him, and the Sewer's account of what they might have expected if they had! Here's the Sewer, here's the Sewer! Here's the wide-awake Sewer; always on the look-out; the leading Journal of the United States, now in its twelfth thousand, and still a-printing off. Here's the New York Sewer!'

'It is in such enlightened means,' said a voice almost in Martin's ear, 'that the bubbling passions of my country find a vent.'

---

56. A patriot

CHAPTER 16

He was a great politician; and the one article of his creed, in reference to all public obligations involving the good faith and integrity of his country, was, 'run a moist pen slick through everything, and start fresh.' This made him a patriot. In commercial affairs he was a bold speculator. In plainer words he had a most distinguished genius for swindling, and could start a bank, or negotiate a loan, or form a land-jobbing company (entailing ruin, pestilence, and death, on hundreds of families), with any gifted creature in the Union. This made him an admirable man of business. He could hang about a bar-room, discussing the affairs of the nation, for twelve hours together; and in that time could hold forth with more intolerable dulness, chew more tobacco, smoke more tobacco, drink more rum-toddy, mint-julep, gin-sling, and cock-tail, than any private gentleman of his acquaintance. This made him an orator and a man of the people. In a word, the major was a rising character, and a popular character, and was in a fair way to be sent by the popular party to the State House of New York, if not in the end to Washington itself. But as a man's private prosperity does not always keep pace with his patriotic devotion to public affairs; and as fraudulent transactions have their downs as well as ups, the major was occasionally under a cloud. Hence, just now, Mrs. Pawkins kept a boarding-house, and Major Pawkins rather 'loafed' his time away than otherwise.

---

57. At table – and afterward

CHAPTER 16

It was a numerous company, eighteen or twenty perhaps. Of these some five or six were ladies, who sat wedged together in a little phalanx by themselves. All the knives and forks were working away at a rate that was quite alarming; very few words were spoken; and everybody seemed to eat his utmost in self-defence, as if a famine were expected to set in before breakfast time to-morrow morning, and it had become high time to assert the first law of nature. The poultry, which may perhaps be considered to have formed the staple of the entertainment – for there was a turkey at the top, a pair of ducks at the bottom, and two fowls in the middle – disappeared as rapidly as if every bird had had the use of its wings, and had flown in desperation down a human throat. The oysters, stewed and pickled, leaped from their capacious reservoirs, and slid by scores into the mouths of the assembly. The sharpest pickles vanished, whole cucumbers at once, like sugar-plums, and no man winked his eye. Great heaps of indigestible matter melted away as ice before the sun. It was a solemn and an awful thing to see. Dyspeptic individuals bolted their food in wedges; feeding, not themselves, but broods of nightmares, who were continually standing at livery within them. Spare men, with lank and rigid cheeks, came out unsatisfied from the destruction of heavy dishes, and glared with watchful eyes upon the pastry. What Mrs. Pawkins felt each day at dinner-time is hidden from all human knowledge. But she had one comfort. It was very soon over.

.   .   .   .

Several of the gentlemen got up, one by one, and walked off as they swallowed their last morsel; pausing generally by the stove for a minute or so to refresh themselves at the brass spittoons. A few sedentary characters, however, remained at table full a quarter of an hour, and did not rise until the ladies rose, when all stood up.

'Where are they going?' asked Martin, in the ear of Mr. Jefferson Brick.

'To their bedrooms, sir.'

'Is there no dessert, or other interval of conversation?' asked Martin, who was disposed to enjoy himself after his long voyage.

'We are a busy people here, sir, and have no time for that,' was the reply.

So the ladies passed out in single file; Mr. Jefferson Brick and such other married gentlemen as were left, acknowledging the departure of their other halves by a nod; and there was an end of *them*. Martin thought this an uncomfortable custom, but he kept his opinion to himself for the present, being anxious to hear, and inform himself by, the conversation of the busy gentlemen, who now lounged about the stove as if a great weight had been taken off their minds by the withdrawal of the other sex; and who made a plentiful use of the spittoons and their toothpicks.

It was rather barren of interest, to say the truth; and the greater part of it may be summed up in one word. Dollars. All their cares, hopes, joys, affections, virtues, and associations, seemed to be melted down into dollars. Whatever the chance contributions that fell into the slow cauldron of their talk, they made the gruel thick and slab with dollars. Men were weighed by their dollars, measures gauged by their dollars; life was auctioneered, appraised, put up, and knocked down for its dollars. The next respectable thing to dollars was any venture having their attainment for its end. The more of that worthless ballast, honour and fair-dealing, which any man cast overboard from the ship of his Good Name and Good Intent, the more ample stowage-room he had for dollars. Make commerce one huge lie and mighty theft. Deface the banner of the nation for an idle rag; pollute it star by star; and cut out stripe by stripe as from the arm of a degraded soldier. Do anything for dollars! What is a flag to *them*!

---

58. A cultivated family

CHAPTER 17

Another delightful circumstance turned up before the first cup of tea was drunk. The whole family had been in England. There was a pleasant thing! But Martin was not quite so glad of this, when he found that they knew all the great dukes, lords, viscounts, marquesses, duchesses, knights, and baronets, quite affectionately, and were beyond everything interested in the least particular concerning them. However, when they asked after the wearer of this or that coronet, and said, 'Was he quite well?' Martin answered, 'Yes, oh yes. Never better;' and when they said, 'his lordship's mother, the duchess, was she much changed?' Martin said, 'Oh dear no, they would know her anywhere, if they saw her to-morrow;' and so got on pretty well. In like manner when the young ladies questioned him touching the Gold Fish in that Grecian fountain in such and such a nobleman's conservatory, and whether there were as many as there used to be, he gravely reported, after mature consideration, that there must be at least twice as many: and as to the exotics, 'Oh, well! it was of no use talking about *them*; they must be seen to be believed;' which improved state of circumstances reminded the family of the splendour of that brilliant festival (comprehending the whole British Peerage and Court Calendar) to which they were specially invited, and which indeed had been partly given in their honour: and recollections of what Mr. Norris the father had said to the marquess, and of what Mrs. Norris the mother had said to the marchioness, and of what the marquess and the marchioness had both said, when they said that upon their words and honours they wished Mr. Norris the father and Mrs. Norris the mother, and the Misses Norris the daughters, and Mr. Norris Junior, the son, would only take up their permanent residence in England, and give them the pleasure of their everlasting friendship, occupied a very considerable time.

59. A social catastrophe

CHAPTER 17

To be sure, it would have been impossible for the family to testify purer delight and joy than at this unlooked-for appearance of General Fladdock! The general was as warmly received as if New York had been in a state of siege and no other general was to be got for love or money. He shook hands with the Norrises three times all round, and then reviewed them from a little distance as a brave commander might, with his ample cloak drawn forward over the right shoulder and thrown back upon the left side to reveal his manly breast.

'And do I then,' cried the general, 'once again behold the choicest spirits of my country!'

'Yes,' said Mr. Norris the father. 'Here we are, general.'

Then all the Norrises pressed round the general, inquiring how and where he had been since the date of his letter, and how he had enjoyed himself in foreign parts, and particularly and above all, to what extent he had become acquainted with the great dukes, lords, viscounts, marquesses, duchesses, knights, and baronets, in whom the people of those benighted countries had delight.

'Well then, don't ask me,' said the general, holding up his hand. 'I was among 'em all the time, and have got public journals in my trunk with my name printed:' he lowered his voice and was very impressive here: 'among the fashionable news. But, oh the conventionalities of that a-mazing Eu–rope!'

'Ah!' cried Mr. Norris the father, giving his head a melancholy shake, and looking towards Martin as though he would say, 'I can't deny it, sir. I would if I could.'

'The limited diffusion of a moral sense in that country!' exclaimed the general. 'The absence of a moral dignity in man!'

'Ah!' sighed all the Norrises, quite overwhelmed with despondency.

'I couldn't have realised it,' pursued the general, 'without being located on the spot. Norris, your imagination is the imagination of a strong man, but *you* couldn't have realised it, without being located on the spot!'

'Never,' said Mr. Norris.

'The ex-clusiveness, the pride, the form, the ceremony,' exclaimed the general, emphasising the article more vigorously at every repetition. 'The artificial barriers set up between man and man; the division of the human race into court cards and plain cards, of every denomination – into clubs, diamonds, spades, anything but hearts!'

'Ah!' cried the whole family. 'Too true, general!'

'But stay!' cried Mr. Norris the father, taking him by the arm. 'Surely you crossed in the Screw, general?'

'Well! so I did,' was the reply.

'Possible!' cried the young ladies. 'Only think!'

The general seemed at a loss to understand why his having come home in the Screw should occasion such a sensation, nor did he seem at all clearer on the subject when Mr. Norris, introducing him to Martin, said:

'A fellow-passenger of yours, I think?'

'Of mine?' exclaimed the general; 'No!'

He had never seen Martin, but Martin had seen him, and recognised him, now that they stood face to face, as the gentleman who had stuck his hands in his pockets towards the end of the voyage, and walked the deck with his nostrils dilated.

Everybody looked at Martin. There was no help for it. The truth must out.

"On Board the 'Screw,'" from Martin Chuzzlewit

'I came over in the same ship as the general,' said Martin, 'but not in the same cabin. It being necessary for me to observe strict economy, I took my passage in the steerage.'

If the general had been carried up bodily to a loaded cannon, and required to let it off that moment, he could not have been in a state of greater consternation than when he heard these words. He, Fladdock, Fladdock in full militia uniform, Fladdock the General, Fladdock the caressed of foreign noblemen, expected to know a fellow who had come over in the steerage of a line-of-packet ship, at the cost of four pound ten! And meeting that fellow in the very sanctuary of New York fashion, and nestling in the bosom of the New York aristocracy! He almost laid his hand upon his sword.

A death-like stillness fell upon the Norrises. If this story should get wind, their country relation had, by his imprudence, for ever disgraced them. They were the bright particular stars of an exalted New York sphere. There were other fashionable spheres above them, and other fashionable spheres below, and none of the stars in any one of these spheres had anything to say to the stars in any other of these spheres. But, through all the spheres it would go forth, that the Norrises, deceived by gentlemanly manners and appearances, had, falling from their high estate, 'received' a dollarless and unknown man. O guardian eagle of the pure Republic, had they lived for this!

'You will allow me,' said Martin, after a terrible silence, 'to take my leave. I feel that I am the cause of at least as much embarrassment here, as I have brought upon myself. But I am bound, before I go, to exonerate this gentleman, who, in introducing me to such society, was quite ignorant of my unworthiness, I assure you.'

With that he made his bow to the Norrises, and walked out like a man of snow: very cool externally, but pretty hot within.

'Come, come,' said Mr. Norris the father, looking with a pale face on the assembled circle as Martin closed the door, 'the young man has this night beheld a refinement of social manner, and an easy magnificence of social decoration, to which he is a stranger in his own country. Let us hope it may awake a moral sense within him.'

60. Feminine pastimes

CHAPTER 17

These ladies were all three talking together in a very loud tone when Martin and his friend entered; but seeing those gentlemen, they stopped directly, and became excessively genteel, not to say frosty. As they went on to exchange some few remarks in whispers, the very water in the tea-pot might have fallen twenty degrees in temperature beneath their chilling coldness.

'Have you been to meeting, Mrs. Brick?' asked Martin's friend, with something of a roguish twinkle in his eye.

'To lecture, sir.'

'I beg your pardon. I forgot. You don't go to meeting, I think?'

Here the lady on the right of Mrs. Brick gave a pious cough, as much as to say '*I* do!' As, indeed, she did nearly every night in the week.

'A good discourse, ma'am?' asked Mr. Bevan, addressing this lady.

The lady raised her eyes in a pious manner, and answered 'Yes.' She had been much comforted by some good, strong, peppery doctrine, which satisfactorily disposed of all her friends and acquaintances, and quite settled *their* business. Her bonnet, too, had far outshone every bonnet in the congregation: so she was tranquil on all accounts.

'What course of lectures are you attending now, ma'am?' said Martin's friend, turning again to Mrs. Brick.

'The Philosophy of the Soul, on Wednesdays.'

'On Mondays?'

'The Philosophy of Crime.'

'On Fridays?'

'The Philosophy of Vegetables.'

'You have forgotten Thursdays; the Philosophy of Government, my dear,' observed the third lady.

'No,' said Mrs. Brick. 'That's Tuesdays.'

'So it is!' cried the lady. 'The Philosophy of Matter on Thursdays, of course.'

'You see, Mr. Chuzzlewit, our ladies are fully employed,' said Bevan.

'Indeed you have reason to say so,' answered Martin. 'Between these very grave pursuits abroad, and family duties at home, their time must be pretty well engrossed.'

Martin stopped here, for he saw that the ladies regarded him with no very great favour, though what he had done to deserve the disdainful expression which appeared in their faces he was at a loss to divine. But on their going up-stairs to their bedrooms: which they very soon did: Mr. Bevan informed him that domestic drudgery was far beneath the exalted range of these Philosophers, and that the chances were a hundred to one that not one of the three could perform the easiest woman's work for herself, or make the simplest article of dress for any of her children.

---

61. Martin instructed regarding his Queen's habitation

CHAPTER 21

'Well!' resumed their new friend, after staring at them intently during the whole interval of silence: 'how's the unnat'ral old parent by this time?'

Mr. Tapley regarding this inquiry as only another version of the impertinent English question, 'How's your mother?' would have resented it instantly, but for Martin's prompt interposition.

'You mean the old country?' he said.

'Ah!' was the reply. 'How's she? Progressing back'ards, I expect, as usual? Well! How's Queen Victoria?'

'In good health, I believe,' said Martin.

'Queen Victoria won't shake in her royal shoes at all, when she hears to-morrow named,' observed the stranger. 'No.'

'Not that I am aware of. Why should she?'

'She won't be taken with a cold chill, when she realises what is being done in these diggings,' said the stranger. 'No.'

'No,' said Martin. 'I think I could take my oath on that.'

The strange gentleman looked at him as if in pity for his ignorance or prejudice, and said:

'Well, sir, I tell you this – there ain't a ĕn-gīne with its biler bust, in God A'mighty's free U-nited States, so fixed, and nipped, and frizzled to a most e-tarnal smash, as that young critter, in her luxurious location in the Tower of London, will be, when she reads the next double-extra Watertoast Gazette.'

Several other gentlemen had left their seats and gathered round during the foregoing dialogue. They were highly delighted with this speech. One very lank gentleman, in a loose limp white cravat, long white waistcoat, and a black great-coat, who seemed to be in authority among them, felt called upon to acknowledge it.

'Hem! Mr. La Fayette Kettle,' he said, taking off his hat.

There was a grave murmur of 'Hush!'

'Mr. La Fayette Kettle! Sir!'

Mr. Kettle bowed.

'In the name of this company, sir, and in the name of our common country, and in the name of that righteous cause of holy sympathy in which we are engaged, I thank you. I thank you, sir, in the name of the Watertoast Sympathisers; and I thank you, sir, in the name of the Watertoast Gazette; and I thank you, sir, in the name of the star-spangled banner of the Great United States, for your eloquent and categorical exposition. And if, sir,' said the speaker, poking Martin with the handle of his umbrella to bespeak his attention, for he was listening to a whisper from Mark; 'if, sir, in such a place, and at such a time, I might venture to con-clude with a sentiment, glancing – however slantin'dicularly – at the subject in hand, I would say, sir, may the British Lion have his talons eradicated by the noble bill of the American Eagle, and be taught to play upon the Irish Harp and the Scotch Fiddle that music which is breathed in every empty shell that lies upon the shores of green Co-lumbia!'

Here the lank gentleman sat down again, amidst a great sensation; and every one looked very grave.

'General Choke,' said Mr. La Fayette Kettle, 'you warm my heart; sir, you warm my heart. But the British Lion is not unrepresented here, sir; and I should be glad to hear his answer to those remarks.'

'Upon my word,' cried Martin, laughing, 'since you do me the honour to consider me his representative, I have only to say that I never heard of Queen Victoria reading the What's-his-name Gazette, and that I should scarcely think it probable.'

General Choke smiled upon the rest, and said, in patient and benignant explanation:

'It is sent to her, sir. It is sent to her. Per mail.'

'But if it is addressed to the Tower of London, it would hardly come to hand, I fear,' returned Martin: 'for she don't live there.'

'The Queen of England, gentlemen,' observed Mr. Tapley, affecting the greatest politeness, and regarding them with an immovable face, 'usually lives in the Mint to take care of the money. She *has* lodgings, in virtue of her office, with the Lord Mayor at the Mansion-House; but don't often occupy them, in consequence of the parlour chimney smoking.'

'Mark,' said Martin, 'I shall be very much obliged to you if you'll have the goodness not to interfere with preposterous statements, however jocose they may appear to you. I was merely remarking, gentlemen – though it's a point of very little import – that the Queen of England does not happen to live in the Tower of London.'

'General!' cried Mr. La Fayette Kettle. 'You hear?'

'General!' echoed several others. 'General!'

'Hush! Pray, silence!' said General Choke, holding up his hand, and speaking with a patient and complacent benevolence that was quite touching. 'I have always remarked it as a very extraordinary circumstance, which I impute to the natur' of British Institutions and their tendency to suppress that popular inquiry and information which air so widely diffused even in the trackless forests of this vast Continent of the Western Ocean; that the knowledge of the Britishers themselves on such points is not to be compared with that possessed by our intelligent and locomotive citizens. This is interesting, and confirms my observation. When you say, sir,' he continued, addressing Martin, 'that your Queen does not reside in the Tower of London, you fall into an error, not uncommon to your countrymen, even when their abilities and moral elements air such as to command respect. But, sir, you air wrong. She *does* live there – '

'When she is at the Court of Saint James's;' interposed Kettle.

'When she is at the Court of Saint James's, of course,' returned the General, in the same benignant way: 'for if her location was in Windsor Pavilion it couldn't be in London at the same time. Your Tower of London, sir,' pursued the General, smiling with a mild consciousness of his knowledge, 'is nat'rally your royal residence. Being located in the immediate neighbourhood of your Parks, your Drives, your Triumphant Arches, your Opera, and your Royal Almacks, it nat'rally suggests itself as the place for holding a luxurious and thoughtless court. And, consequently,' said the General, 'consequently, the court is held there.'

---

62. The Watertoast Sympathisers

CHAPTER 21

In his preface to the Cheap Edition (1852) of Chuzzlewit, *Dickens stated that this description of the Watertoast Association was "a literal paraphrase of some reports of public proceedings in the United States (especially of the proceedings of a certain Brandywine Association), which were printed in The Times Newspaper in June and July 1843." The Horse Guards building (erected 1753) stands in Whitehall, London; its clock, Walter Thornbury notes in his* Old and New London *(vol. 3, p. 386), "has always been regarded as an authority for its correctness; inasmuch as to render it the grand regulator of all the timepieces in London in its vicinity." The "Public Man in Ireland" was Daniel O'Connell, tireless campaigner for Irish Home Rule.*

'Well, sir!' he said, as he shook hands with Martin, 'here is a spectacle calc'lated to make the British Lion put his tail between his legs, and howl with anguish, I expect!'

Martin certainly thought it possible that the British Lion might have been rather out of his element in that Ark: but he kept the idea to himself. The General was then voted to the chair, on the motion of a pallid lad of the Jefferson Brick school: who forthwith set in for a high-spiced speech, with a good deal about hearths and homes in it, and unriveting the chains of Tyranny.

Oh but it was a clincher for the British Lion, it was! The indignation of the glowing young Columbian knew no bounds. If he could only have been one of his own forefathers, he said, wouldn't he have peppered that same Lion, and been to him as another Brute Tamer with a wire whip, teaching him lessons not easily forgotten. 'Lion! (cried that young Columbian) where is he? Who is he? What is he? Show him to me. Let me have him here. Here!' said the young Columbian, in a wrestling attitude, 'upon this sacred altar. Here!' cried the young Columbian, idealising the dining-table, 'upon ancestral ashes, cemented with the glorious blood poured out like water on our native plains of Chickabiddy Lick! Bring forth that Lion!' said the young Columbian. 'Alone, I dare him! I taunt that Lion. I tell that Lion, that Freedom's hand once twisted in his mane, he rolls a corse before me, and the Eagles of the Great Republic laugh ha, ha!'

When it was found that the Lion didn't come, but kept out of the way; that the young Columbian stood there, with folded arms, alone in

"The British Lion Disarmed," by Thomas Nast, 1 August 1868. The cartoon refers to the dispute of Great Britain and the United States over damages caused by British-financed Confederate ships during the Civil War

his glory; and consequently that the Eagles were no doubt laughing wildly on the mountain tops; such cheers arose as might have shaken the hands upon the Horse-Guards' clock, and changed the very mean time of the day in England's capital.

'Who is this?' Martin telegraphed to La Fayette.

The Secretary wrote something, very gravely, on a piece of paper, twisted it up, and had it passed to him from hand to hand. It was an improvement on the old sentiment: 'Perhaps as remarkable a man as any in our country.'

This young Columbian was succeeded by another, to the full as eloquent as he, who drew down storms of cheers. But both remarkable youths, in their great excitement (for your true poetry can never stoop to details), forgot to say with whom or what the Watertoasters sympathised, and likewise why or wherefore they were sympathetic. Thus Martin remained for a long time as completely in the dark as ever; until at length a ray of light broke in upon him through the medium of the Secretary, who, by reading the minutes of their past proceedings, made the matter somewhat clearer. He then learned that the Watertoast Association sympathised with a certain Public Man in Ireland, who held a contest upon certain points with England: and that they did so, because they didn't love England at all – not by any means because they loved Ireland much; being indeed horribly jealous and distrustful of its people always, and only tolerating them because of their working hard, which made them very useful; labour being held in greater indignity in the simple republic than in any other country upon earth.

63. Martin lionised

CHAPTER 22

"Mr. Miller" was Joe Miller (1684–1738), a very popular English low comedian, the supposed author of a collection of jocose anecdotes entitled Joe Miller's Jestbook, *published the year after his death.*

The first notification he received of this change in his position, was the following epistle, written in a thin running hand, – with here and there a fat letter or two, to make the general effect more striking, – on a sheet of paper, ruled with blue lines.

'*National Hotel, Monday Morning.*

'Dear Sir,

'When I had the privillidge of being your fellow-traveller in the cars, the day before yesterday, you offered some remarks upon the subject of the Tower of London, which (in common with my fellow-citizens generally) I could wish to hear repeated to a public audience.

'As secretary to the Young Men's Watertoast Association of this town, I am requested to inform you that the Society will be proud to hear you deliver a lecture upon the Tower of London, at their Hall to-morrow evening, at seven o'clock; and as a large issue of quarter-dollar tickets may be expected, your answer and consent by bearer will be considered obliging.

'Dear Sir, yours truly,

'La Fayette Kettle.

'The Honourable Mr. Chuzzlewit.

'P.S. – The Society would not be particular in limiting you to the Tower of London. Permit me to suggest that any remarks upon the Elements of Geology, or (if more convenient) upon the Writings of your talented and witty countryman, the honourable Mr. Miller, would be well received.'

Very much aghast at this invitation, Martin wrote back, civilly declining it; and had scarcely done so, when he received another letter.

'(Private).

'*No. 47, Bunker Hill Street, Monday Morning.*

'Sir,

'I was raised in those interminable solitudes where our mighty Mississippi (or Father of Waters) rolls his turbid flood.

'I am young, and ardent. For there is a poetry in wildness, and every alligator basking in the slime is in himself an Epic, self-contained. I aspire for fame. It is my yearning and my thirst.

'Are you, sir, aware of any member of Congress in England, who would undertake to pay my expenses to that country, and for six months after my arrival?

'There is something within me which gives me the assurance that this enlightened patronage would not be thrown away. In literature or art; the bar, the pulpit, or the stage; in one or other, if not all, I feel that I am certain to succeed.

'If too much engaged to write to any such yourself, please let me have a list of three or four of those most likely to respond, and I will address them through the Post Office. May I also ask you to favour me with any critical observations that have ever presented themselves to your reflective faculties, on "Cain: a Mystery," by the Right Honourable Lord Byron?

'I am, Sir,
'Yours (forgive me if I add, soaringly),
'PUTNAM SMIF.
'P.S. – Address your answer to America Junior, Messrs. Hancock &
Floby, Dry Goods Store, as above.'

Both of which letters, together with Martin's reply to each, were,
according to a laudable custom, much tending to the promotion of
gentlemanly feeling and social confidence, published in the next number of the Watertoast Gazette.

.   .   .   .

Up they came with a rush. Up they came until the room was full,
and, through the open door, a dismal perspective of more to come,
was shown upon the stairs. One after another, one after another, doz-
en after dozen, score after score, more, more, more, up they came: all
shaking hands with Martin. Such varieties of hands, the thick, the thin,
the short, the long, the fat, the lean, the coarse, the fine; such differences of temperature, the hot, the cold, the dry, the moist, the flabby;
such diversities of grasp, the tight, the loose, the short-lived, and the
lingering! Still up, up, up, more, more, more: and ever and anon the
Captain's voice was heard above the crowd: 'There's more below!
there's more below. Now, gentlemen, you that have been introduced
to Mr. Chuzzlewit, will you clear, gentlemen? Will you clear? Will
you be so good as clear, gentlemen, and make a little room for more?'
Regardless of the Captain's cries, they didn't clear at all, but stood
there, bolt upright and staring. Two gentlemen connected with the
Watertoast Gazette had come express to get the matter for an article
on Martin. They had agreed to divide the labour. One of them took
him below the waistcoat; one above. Each stood directly in front of
his subject with his head a little on one side, intent on his department.
If Martin put one boot before the other, the lower gentleman was
down upon him; he rubbed a pimple on his nose, and the upper gentleman booked it. He opened his mouth to speak, and the same gentleman
was on one knee before him, looking in at his teeth, with the nice
scrutiny of a dentist. Amateurs in the physiognomical and phrenological sciences roved about him with watchful eyes and itching fingers,
and sometimes one, more daring than the rest, made a mad grasp at
the back of his head, and vanished in the crowd. They had him in all
points of view: in front, in profile, three-quarter face, and behind.
Those who were not professional or scientific, audibly exchanged
opinions on his looks. New lights shone in upon him, in respect of his
nose. Contradictory rumours were abroad on the subject of his hair.
And still the Captain's voice was heard – so stifled by the concourse,

that he seemed to speak from underneath a feather-bed, exclaiming, 'Gentlemen, you that have been introduced to Mr. Chuzzlewit, *will* you clear?'

Even when they began to clear it was no better; for then a stream of gentlemen, every one with a lady on each arm (exactly like the chorus to the National Anthem when Royalty goes in state to the play), came gliding in: every new group fresher than the last, and bent on staying to the latest moment. If they spoke to him, which was not often, they invariably asked the same questions, in the same tone: with no more remorse, or delicacy, or consideration, than if he had been a figure of stone, purchased, and paid for, and set up there for their delight. Even when, in the slow course of time, these died off, it was as bad as ever, if not worse; for then the boys grew bold, and came in as a class of themselves, and did everything that the grown-up people had done. Uncouth stragglers, too, appeared; men of a ghostly kind, who being in, didn't know how to get out again: insomuch that one silent gentleman with glazed and fishy eyes, and only one button on his waistcoat (which was a very large metal one, and shone prodigiously), got behind the door, and stood there, like a clock, long after everybody else was gone.

---

64. National self-justification

CHAPTER 22

An "Orson" is a wild man of the woods. The name comes from the medieval French romance of the twin brothers Valentine and Orson; the latter was carried off by a bear after the brothers' birth in the Forest of Orleans.

It is no great matter what Mrs. Hominy said, save that she had learnt it from the cant of a class, and a large class, of her fellow-countrymen, who, in their every word, avow themselves to be as senseless to the high principles on which America sprang, a nation, into life, as any Orson in her legislative halls. Who are no more capable of feeling, or of caring if they did feel, that by reducing their own country to the ebb of honest men's contempt, they put in hazard the rights of nations yet unborn, and very progress of the human race, than are the swine who wallow in their streets. Who think that crying out to other nations, old in their iniquity, 'We are no worse than you!' (No worse!) is high defence and 'vantage-ground enough for that Republic, but yesterday let loose upon her noble course, and but to-day so maimed and lame, so full of sores and ulcers, foul to the eye and almost hopeless to the sense, that her best friends turn from the loathsome creature with disgust. Who, having by their ancestors declared and won their Independence, because they would not bend the knee to certain Public vices and corruptions, and would not abrogate the truth, run riot in the Bad, and turn their backs upon the Good; and lying down contented with the wretched boast that other Temples also are of glass, and stones which batter theirs may be flung back; show themselves, in that alone, as immeasurably behind the import of the trust they hold, and as unworthy to possess it as if the sordid hucksterings of all their little governments – each one a kingdom in its small depravity – were brought into a heap for evidence against them.

---

65. The settlement of Eden

CHAPTER 2 3

Dickens scholars are generally agreed that the novelist's "Eden" was inspired by his sight of the settlement of Cairo, Illinois, in 1842.

He stole out gently, for his companion was sleeping now; and having refreshed himself by washing in the river, where it flowed before the door, took a rough survey of the settlement. There were not above a score of cabins in the whole; half of these appeared untenanted; all were rotten and decayed. The most tottering, abject, and forlorn among them was called, with great propriety, the Bank, and National Credit Office. It had some feeble props about it, but was settling deep down in the mud, past all recovery.

Here and there an effort had been made to clear the land, and something like a field had been marked out, where, among the stumps and ashes of burnt trees, a scanty crop of Indian corn was growing. In some quarters, a snake or zigzag fence had been begun, but in no instance had it been completed; and the fallen logs, half hidden in the soil, lay mouldering away. Three or four meagre dogs, wasted and vexed with hunger; some long-legged pigs, wandering away into the woods in search of food; some children, nearly naked, gazing at him from the huts; were all the living things he saw. A fetid vapour, hot and sickening as the breath of an oven, rose up from the earth, and hung on everything around; and as his foot-prints sunk into the marshy ground, a black ooze started forth to blot them out.

Their own land was mere forest. The trees had grown so thick and

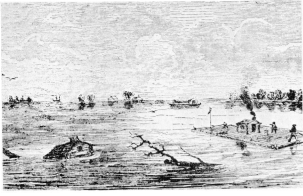

close that they shouldered one another out of their places, and the
weakest, forced into shapes of strange distortion, languished like crip-
ples. The best were stunted, from the pressure and the want of room;
and high about the stems of all grew long rank grass, dank weeds, and
frowsy underwood: not divisible into their separate kinds, but tangled
all together in a heap; a jungle deep and dark, with neither earth nor
water at its roots, but putrid matter, formed of the pulpy offal of the
two, and of their own corruption.

66. A child of Freedom

CHAPTER 33

Mr. Chollop was, of course, one of the most remarkable men in the
country; but he really was a notorious person besides. He was usually
described by his friends, in the South and West, as 'a splendid sample

of our na-tive raw material, sir,' and was much esteemed for his devotion to rational Liberty; for the better propagation whereof he usually
carried a brace of revolving-pistols in his coat pocket, with seven barrels a-piece. He also carried, amongst other trinkets, a sword-stick,
which he called his 'Tickler;' and a great knife, which (for he was a
man of a pleasant turn of humour) he called 'Ripper', in allusion to its
usefulness as a means of ventilating the stomach of any adversary in a
close contest. He had used these weapons with distinguished effect in
several instances, all duly chronicled in the newspapers; and was greatly beloved for the gallant manner in which he had 'jobbed out' the
eye of one gentleman, as he was in the act of knocking at his own
street-door.

Mr. Chollop was a man of a roving disposition; and, in any less advanced community, might have been mistaken for a violent vagabond.
But his fine qualities being perfectly understood and appreciated in
those regions where his lot was cast, and where he had many kindred
spirits to consort with, he may be regarded as having been born under
a fortunate star, which is not always the case with a man so much before the age in which he lives. Preferring, with a view to the gratification of his tickling and ripping fancies, to dwell upon the outskirts of
society, and in the more remote towns and cities, he was in the habit
of emigrating from place to place, and establishing in each some business – usually a newspaper – which he presently sold: for the most
part closing the bargain by challenging, stabbing, pistolling, or gouging the new editor, before he had quite taken possession of the property.

He had come to Eden on a speculation of this kind, but had abandoned it, and was about to leave. He always introduced himself to
strangers as a worshipper of Freedom; was the consistent advocate of
Lynch law, and slavery; and invariably recommended, both in print
and speech, the 'tarring and feathering' of any unpopular person who
differed from himself. He called this 'planting the standard of civilisation in the wilder gardens of My country.'

There is little doubt that Chollop would have planted this standard
in Eden at Mark's expense, in return for his plainness of speech (for
the genuine Freedom is dumb, save when she vaunts herself), but for
the utter desolation and decay prevailing in the settlement, and his
own approaching departure from it. As it was, he contented himself
with showing Mark one of the revolving-pistols, and asking him what
he thought of that weapon.

'It ain't long since I shot a man down with that, sir, in the State of
Illin*oy*,' observed Chollop.

'Did you, indeed!' said Mark, without the smallest agitation. 'Very
free of you. And very independent!'

'I shot him down, sir,' pursued Chollop, 'for asserting in the Spartan Portico, a tri-weekly journal, that the ancient Athenians went a-head of the present Locofoco Ticket.'

'And what's that?' asked Mark.

'Europian not to know,' said Chollop, smoking placidly. 'Europian quite!'

.   .   .   .

'Afore I go,' he said sternly, 'I have got a leetle word to say to you. You are darnnation 'cute, you are.'

Mark thanked him for the compliment.

'But you are much too 'cute to last. I can't con-ceive of any spotted Painter in the bush, as ever was so riddled through and through as you will be, I bet.'

'What for?' asked Mark.

'We must be cracked-up, sir,' retorted Chollop, in a tone of menace. 'You are not now in A despotic land. We are a model to the airth, and must be jist cracked-up, I tell you.'

'What! I speak too free, do I?' cried Mark.

'I have draw'd upon A man, and fired upon A man for less,' said Chollop, frowning. 'I have know'd strong men obleeged to make themselves uncommon skase for less. I have know'd men Lynched for less, and beaten into punkin'-sarse for less, by an enlightened people. We are the intellect and virtue of the airth, the cream Of human natur', and the flower Of moral force. Our backs is easy ris. We must be cracked-up, or they rises, and we snarls. We shows our teeth, I tell you, fierce. You'd better crack us up, you had!'

After the delivery of this caution, Mr. Chollop departed; with Ripper, Tickler, and the revolvers, all ready for action on the shortest notice.

---

67. The Pogram Defiance

CHAPTER 34

'You air fortunate, sir, in having an opportunity of beholding our Elijah Pogram, sir.'

'Your Elijahpogram!' said Martin, thinking it was all one word, and a building of some sort.

'Yes, sir.'

Martin tried to look as if he understood him, but he couldn't make it out.

'Yes, sir,' repeated the gentleman. 'Our Elijah Pogram, sir, is, at this minute, identically settin' by the en-gine biler.'

The gentleman under the umbrella put his right forefinger to his eyebrow, as if he were revolving schemes of state.

'That is Elijah Pogram, is it?' said Martin.

'Yes, sir,' replied the other. 'That is Elijah Pogram.'

'Dear me!' said Martin. 'I am astonished.' But he had not the least idea who this Elijah Pogram was; having never heard the name in all his life.

'If the biler of this vessel was Toe bust, sir,' said his new acquaintance, 'and Toe bust now, this would be a festival day in the calendar of despotism; pretty nigh equallin', sir, in its effects upon the human race, our Fourth of glorious July. Yes, sir, that is the Honourable Elijah Pogram, Member of Congress; one of the master-minds of our country, sir. There is a brow, sir, there!'

'Quite remarkable,' said Martin.

'Yes, sir. Our own immortal Chiggle, sir, is said to have observed, when he made the celebrated Pogram statter in marble, which rose so much con-test and preju-dice in Europe, that the brow was more than mortal. This was before the Pogram Defiance, and was, therefore, a pre-diction, cruel smart.'

'What is the Pogram Defiance?' asked Martin, thinking, perhaps, it was the sign of a public-house.

'An o-ration, sir,' returned his friend.

'Oh, to be sure,' cried Martin. 'What am I thinking of! It defied –'

'It defied the world, sir,' said the other, gravely. 'Defied the world in general to com-pete with our country upon any hook; and devellop'd our internal resources for making war upon the universal airth.'

.   .   .   .

'It is strange,' said Pogram, looking round upon the group, 'this hatred of our country, and her Institutions! This national antipathy is deeply rooted in the British mind!'

'Good Heaven, sir,' cried Martin. 'Is the Eden Land Corporation, with Mr. Scadder at its head, and all the misery it has worked, at its door, an Institution of America? A part of any form of government that ever was known or heard of?'

'I con-sider the cause of this to be,' said Pogram, looking round again and taking himself up where Martin had interrupted him, 'partly jealousy and pre-judice, and partly the nat'ral unfitness of the British people to appreciate the ex-alted Institutions of our native land. I ex-pect, sir,' turning to Martin again, 'that a gentleman named Chollop happened in upon you during your lo-cation in the town of Eden?'

'Yes,' answered Martin; 'but my friend can answer this better than I can, for I was very ill at the time. Mark! The gentleman is speaking of Mr. Chollop.'

'Oh. Yes, sir. Yes. *I* see him,' observed Mark.

'A splendid example of our na-tive raw material, sir?' said Pogram, interrogatively.

'Indeed, sir!' cried Mark.

The Honourable Elijah Pogram glanced at his friends as though he would have said, 'Observe this! See what follows!' and they rendered tribute to the Pogram genius by a gentle murmur.

'Our fellow-countryman is a model of a man, quite fresh from Na-tur's mold!' said Pogram, with enthusiasm. 'He is true-born child of this free hemisphere! Verdant as the mountains of our country; bright and flowing as our mineral Licks; unspiled by withering convention-alities as air our broad and boundless Perearers! Rough he may be. So air our Barrs. Wild he may be. So air our Buffalers. But he is a child of Natur', and a child of Freedom; and his boastful answer to the Despot and the Tyrant is, that his bright home is in the Settin Sun.'

Part of this referred to Chollop, and part to a Western postmaster, who, being a public defaulter not very long before (a character not at all uncommon in America), had been removed from office; and on whose behalf Mr. Pogram (he voted for Pogram) had thundered the last sentence from his seat in Congress, at the head of an unpopular President. It told brilliantly; for the bystanders were delighted, and one of them said to Martin, 'that he guessed he had now seen something of the eloquential aspect of our country, and was chawed up pritty small.'

---

68. Literary ladies

CHAPTER 34

The Gracchi were two notable democratic reformers active in Rome between 130 and 120 B.C., champions of the people against the power of the oligarchic Senate; their devoted mother, Cornelia, lavished every care on their upbringing. The Transcendentalists, who insisted on the supremacy of insight over reason and who were inspired by the German Kantian school of idealistic philosophy, flourished in New England about 1830 to 1850; their most prominent spokesman was Emerson.

A lane was made; and Mrs. Hominy, with the aristocratic stalk, the pocket handkerchief, the clasped hands, and the classical cap, came slowly up it, in a procession of one. Mr. Pogram testified emotions of delight on seeing her, and a general hush prevailed. For it was known that when à woman like Mrs. Hominy encountered a man like Pogram, something interesting must be said.

Their first salutations were exchanged in a voice too low to reach the impatient ears of the throng; but they soon became audible, for Mrs. Hominy felt her position, and knew what was expected of her.

Mrs. H. was hard upon him at first; and put him through a rigid catechism in reference to a certain vote he had given, which she had found it necessary, as the mother of the modern Gracchi, to deprecate in a line by itself, set up expressly for the purpose in German text. But Mr. Pogram evading it by a well-timed allusion to the star-spangled banner, which, it appeared, had the remarkable peculiarity of flouting the breeze whenever it was hoisted where the wind blew, she forgave him. They now enlarged on certain questions of tariff, commercial treaty, boundary, importation and exportation, with great effect. And Mrs. Hominy not only talked, as the saying is, like a book, but actually did talk her own books, word for word.

'My! what is this?' cried Mrs. Hominy, opening a little note which was handed her by her excited gentleman-usher. 'Do tell! oh, well, now! on'y think!'

And then she read aloud, as follows:

'Two literary ladies present their compliments to the mother of the modern Gracchi, and claim her kind introduction, as their talented countrywoman, to the honourable (and distinguished) Elijah Pogram, whom the two L.L.'s have often contemplated in the speaking marble of the soul-subduing Chiggle. On a verbal intimation from the mother of the M.G., that she will comply with the request of the two L.L.'s, they will have the immediate pleasure of joining the galaxy assembled to do honour to the patriotic conduct of a Pogram. It may be another bond of union between the two L.L.'s and the mother of the M.G. to observe, that the two L.L.'s are Transcendental.'

Mrs. Hominy promptly rose, and proceeded to the door, whence she returned, after a minute's interval, with the two L.L.'s, whom she led, through the lane in the crowd, with all that stateliness of deportment which was so remarkably her own, up to the great Elijah Pogram. It was (as the shrill boy cried out in an ecstasy) quite the Last Scene from Coriolanus.

One of the L.L.'s wore a brown wig of uncommon size. Sticking on the forehead of the other, by invisible means, was a massive cameo, in size and shape like the raspberry tart which is ordinarily sold for a penny, representing on its front the Capitol at Washington.

'Miss Toppit and Miss Codger!' said Mrs. Hominy.

'Codger's the lady so often mentioned in the English newspapers, I should think, sir,' whispered Mark. 'The oldest inhabitant as never remembers anything.'

'To be presented to a Pogram,' said Miss Codger, 'by a Hominy, indeed, a thrilling moment is it in its impressiveness on what we call our feelings. But why we call them so, or why impressed they are, or if impressed they are at all, or if at all we are, or if there really is, oh gasping one! a Pogram or a Hominy, or any active principle to which we give those titles, is a topic, Spirit searching, light abandoned, much too vast to enter on, at this unlooked-for crisis.'

'Mind and matter,' said the lady in the wig, 'glide swift into the vortex of immensity. Howls the sublime, and softly sleeps the calm Ideal, in the whispering chambers of Imagination. To hear it, sweet it is. But then, outlaughs the stern philosopher, and saith to the Grotesque, "What ho! arrest for me that Agency. Go, bring it here!" And so the vision fadeth.'

After this, they both took Mr. Pogram by the hand, and pressed it to their lips, as a patriotic palm. That homage paid, the mother of the modern Gracchi called for chairs, and the three literary ladies went to work in earnest, to bring poor Pogram out, and make him show himself in all his brilliant colours.

How Pogram got out of his depth instantly, and how the three L.L.'s were never in theirs, is a piece of history not worth recording. Suffice it, that being all four out of their depths, and all unable to swim, they splashed up words in all directions, and floundered about famously. On the whole, it was considered to have been the severest mental exercise ever heard in the National Hotel. Tears stood in the shrill boy's eyes several times; and the whole company observed that their heads ached with the effort – as well they might.

---

69. The travellers' valediction

CHAPTER 34

Mark Tapley, Martin's servant, pays for their passage back to England by working as a cook on board ship.

Cheerily, lads, cheerily! Anchor weighed. Ship in full sail. Her sturdy bowsprit pointing true to England. America a cloud upon the sea behind them!

'Why, Cook! what are you thinking of so steadily?' said Martin.

'Why, I was a-thinking, sir,' returned Mark, 'that if I was a painter and was called upon to paint the American Eagle, how should I do it?'

'Paint it as like an Eagle as you could, I suppose.'

'No,' said Mark. 'That wouldn't do for me, sir. I should want to draw it like a Bat, for its short-sightedness; like a Bantam, for its bragging; like a Magpie, for its honesty; like a Peacock, for its vanity; like a Ostrich, for its putting its head in the mud, and thinking nobody sees it –'

'And like a Phœnix, for its power of springing from the ashes of its faults and vices, and soaring up anew into the sky!' said Martin. 'Well, Mark. Let us hope so.'

IV. Letters & writings, 1844 to 1855

70. The American press

To W. C. Macready, who was touring in America, 3 January 1844.
Fanny Elssler was a dancer who made a sensationally successful tour
of America in 1840 to 1842.

"Puff-ridden"! Why to be sure they are. The Nation is a miserable
Sindbad, and its boasted press (the braggarts!) the loathsome, foul old
man upon his back. And yet with that extraordinary disregard of

"*The Expert Bar-tender*"

Truth, that monstrous audacity of assertion, which makes a Gentleman in heart so rare a man among the people, they will tell you, and proclaim to the four winds, for repetition here, that they don't heed their ignorant and brutal papers. As if the papers could exist if they didn't heed them! As if a man could live in the United States a month, and not see the whole country is led and driven by a herd of rascals, who are the human lice of God's creation! Let any two of these vagabonds in any town you go to, take it into their heads to make you an object of attack, or to direct the general attention elsewhere, and what avail those wonderful images of passion which you have been all your life perfecting, and which I no more believe the rotten heart of that false land is capable of feeling, otherwise than as a fashion, a fancy, than I believe, or ever did believe, it made a distinction between me and Fanny Elssler, or between her and La Fayette. Pah! I never knew what it was to feel disgust and contempt, 'till I travelled in America.

71. American justice

To Elizabeth Sedgwick, an American educationalist, 15 April 1844. The editors of the Pilgrim Edition *of Dickens' letters note (vol. 4, p. 104) that the case Dickens refers to was that of Amelia Norman, tried in New York in January 1844 for stabbing her seducer; she was "acquitted by a sympathetic jury."*

The case of the interesting lady who stabbed the gentleman is exactly the illustration I should have invented, if I were putting a supposititious case, of one of the many phases in which America differs from other Countries, and does such stupendous and grievous injury to the progress of Free Institutions elsewhere. I mean the readiness of her people to take the Law into their own hands; and their manifest want of confidence in, and want of real respect for, the Institutions which they parade so noisily. In the ordinary course of events in any other civilized country, the Jury in that case *must* have found the lady guilty – inasmuch as they were upon their oaths, and she *did* unquestionably stab the gentleman. So they would have found her guilty, and would have recommended her, in their confidence in the Powers that be, to the Mercy of the authorities, with a perfect reliance on their recommendation being carefully, and honorably, and favorably considered. And as to the Constables applauding, they would have appeared in that character for positively the first and last time: and would very likely (and deservedly) have been clapped into prison to boot, for so far forgetting the dignity and decency of a solemn Court of Justice. In America, the course is what you describe – and in the absence of that respect and confidence of which I have just treated, quite naturally so. But not the less dangerously.

---

72. An American panorama

Published in The Examiner, *16 December 1848. "Banvard's Geographical Panorama of the Mississippi and Missouri Rivers" was being exhibited at the Egyptian Hall in London's Piccadilly this month. John Banvard (1815–1891) began his sketching on the Mississippi in 1840. He painted the scenes on canvas, specially woven at Lowell, Massachusetts, in a purpose-built building in Louisville. The Dictionary of American Biography* notes that *"the fidelity of the portrayal was testified to by a number of Mississippi River captains and pilots" but adds, "Its value was geographical; artistic merit it had little or none." Banvard later painted a similar panorama of the Nile.*

But it is a picture three miles long, which occupies two hours in its passage before the audience. It is a picture of one of the greatest streams in the known world, whose course it follows for upwards of three thousand miles. It is a picture irresistibly impressing the spectator with a conviction of its plain and simple truthfulness, even though that were not guaranteed by the best testimonials. It is an easy means of travelling, night and day, without any inconvenience from climate, steamboat company, or fatigue, from New Orleans to the Yellow Stone Bluffs (or from the Yellow Stone Bluffs to New Orleans, as the case may be), and seeing every town and settlement upon the river's banks, and all the strange wild ways of life that are afloat upon its waters. To see this painting is, in a word, to have a thorough understanding of what the great American river is – except, we believe, in the colour of its water – and to acquire a new power of testing the descriptive accuracy of its best describers.

These three miles of canvas have been painted by one man, and there he is, present, pointing out what he deems most worthy of notice. This is history. Poor, untaught, wholly unassisted, he conceives

Extinct geyser, east fork of the Yellowstone

the idea – a truly American idea – of painting 'the largest picture in the world.' Some capital must be got for the materials, and the acquisition of that is his primary object. First, he starts 'a floating diorama' on the Wabash river, which topples over when people come to see it, and keeps all the company at the pumps for dear life. This entertainment drawing more water than money, and being set upon, besides, by robbers armed with bowie knives and rifles, is abandoned. Then he paints a panorama of Venice, and exhibits it in the West successfully, until it goes down in a steamer on the Western waters. Then he sets up a museum at St. Louis, which fails. Then he comes down to Cincinnati, where he does no better. Then, without a farthing, he rows away on the Ohio in a small boat, and lives, like a wild man, upon nuts; until he sells a revolving pistol which cost him twelve dollars, for five-and-twenty. With the proceeds of this commercial transaction he buys a larger boat, lays in a little store of calicoes and cottons, and rows away again among the solitary settlers along-shore, bartering his goods for bee's wax. Thus, in course of time, he earns enough to buy a little skiff, and go to work upon the largest picture in the world!

In his little skiff he travels thousands of miles, with no companions but his pencil, rifle, and dog, making the preparatory sketches for the largest picture in the world. Those completed, he erects a temporary building at Louisville, Kentucky, in which to paint the largest picture in the world. Without the least help, even in the grinding of his colours or the splitting of the wood for his machinery, he falls to

Letter of testimonial by the Mississippi River captains and pilots

We the undersigned, being officers of steamboats continually plying on the Mississipppi river, have examined Mr. Banvard's great Painting, and take great pleasure in recommending it for its fidelity and truthfulness to nature, and giving a correct delineation of the scenery and peculiar characteristics of this mighty river.

J. JOINER,	Captain.	B. SMITH,	Pilot.
DANIEL DASHIEL,	"	HENRY E. LEE,	"
C. S. CASTLEMAN,	"	N. OSTRANDER,	"
T. COLEMAN,	"	ALEX. BADGER,	"
JAC. DILLON,	"	JOHN CRAWFORD,	"
SAMUEL PENNINGTON,	"	JAS. D. HAMILTON,	"
ELI T. DUSTIN,	"	D. S. HALEY,	"
ROBERT BROWN,	"	JAMES O'NEAL,	"
THOMAS NORTHUP,	"	ELI VANSICKLE,	"
R. DE HART,	"	ALLEN PELL,	"

Over one hundred more names omitted for want of room.

State of Kentucky, ⎱ ss.
City of Louisville. ⎰

I, F. A. KAYE, Mayor of the city of Louisville, do hereby certify, that I am personally acquainted with nearly all of the gentlemen who have certified to the correctness of the great Panorama of the Mississippi river, painted by Mr. John Banvard ; and certify further, that they are all practical navigators of the Mississippi river, and are gentlemen of veracity, and are entitled to full credit as such.

FRED. A. KAYE, Mayor.

work, and keeps at work; maintaining himself meanwhile, and buying more colours, wood, and canvas, by doing odd jobs in the decorative way. At last he finishes the largest picture in the world, and opens it for exhibition on a stormy night, when not a single 'human' comes to see it. Not discouraged yet, he goes about among the boatmen, who are well acquainted with the river, and gives them free admission to the largest picture in the world. The boatmen come to see it, are astonished at it, talk about it. 'Our country' wakes up from a rather sullen doze at Louisville, and comes to see it too. The upshot is, that it succeeds; and here it is in London, with its painter standing on a little platform by its side explaining it; and probably, by this time next year, it and he may be in Timbuctoo.

Few can fail to have some interest in such an adventure and in such an adventurer, and they will both repay it amply. There is a mixture of shrewdness and simplicity in the latter, which is very prepossessing; a modesty, and honesty, and an odd original humour, in his manner of telling what he has to tell, that give it a peculiar relish. The picture itself, as an indisputably true and faithful representation of a wonderful region – wood and water, river and prairie, lonely log hut and clustered city rising in the forest – is replete with interest throughout. Its incidental revelations of the different states of society, yet in transition, prevailing at different points of these three thousand miles – slaves and free republicans, French and Southerners; immigrants from abroad, and restless Yankees and Down-Easters ever steaming somewhere; alligators, store-boats, show-boats, theatre-boats, Indians, buffaloes, deserted tents of extinct tribes, and bodies of dead Braves, with their pale faces turned up to the night sky, lying still and solitary in the wilderness, nearer and nearer to which the outposts of civilisation are approaching with gigantic strides to tread their people down, and erase their very track from the earth's face – teem with suggestive matter. We are not disposed to think less kindly of a country when we see so much of it, although our sense of its immense responsibility may be increased.

---

73. An American in Europe

Published in The Examiner, *21 July 1849. Dickens is reviewing* European Life and Manners, in Familiar Letters to Friends, *by Henry Colman, a noted American agriculturist. William Cobbett (1763–1835) was the author of* Rural Rides *(1830), descriptions of life and agricultural conditions in the English countryside. N. P. Willis (1806–1867) was an American poet and journalist who travelled in Europe as correspondent of the* New York Mirror; *his gossipy letters to the paper, publicising domestic details of his hosts in England such as Dickens' friend, Lady Blessington, were published as* Pencillings by the Way *in 1835. Dickens' Shakespearean quotation is adapted from Hotspur's speech in* Henry IV: Part One, *act 1, scene 3.*

Why an honest republican, coming from the United States to England on a mission of inquiry into ploughs, turnips, mangel-wurzel, and live stock, cannot be easy unless he is for ever exhibiting himself to his admiring countrymen, with a countess hanging on each arm, a duke or two walking deferentially behind, and a few old English barons (all his very particular friends) going on before, we cannot, to our satisfaction, comprehend. Neither is his facility of getting into such company quite intelligible; unless something of the spirit which rushes into print with a record of these genteel processions, pervades the aristocratic as well as the republican breast, and tickles the noble fancy with a bird's-eye view of some thousands of American readers across the water, poring, with open mouths and goggle-eyes, over descriptions of its owner's domestic magnificence. We are bound to confess, in justice to a stranger with Mr. Colman's opportunities, that we are not altogether free from a suspicion of this kind.

Mr. Colman came here, as we have already intimated, charged with a mission of inquiry into the general agricultural condition of the country. In this capacity he wrote some reports very creditable to his good sense, expressed in plain nervous English, and testifying to his acquaintance with the rural writings of Cobbett. It would have been better for Mr. Colman, and more agreeable, we conceive, for all Americans of good sense and good taste, if he had contented himself with such authorship; but in an evil hour he committed the two volumes before us, in which

> He talks so like a waiting gentlewoman,
> Of napkins, forks, and spoons (God save the mark!)

– that the dedication of his book to Lady Byron is an obvious mistake, and an outrage on the rights of Mr. N. P. Willis.

---

74. A new issue of *American Notes*

Preface to the Cheap Edition of American Notes, *1850. In the penultimate paragraph Dickens is referring to Galileo before the Spanish Inquisition.*

It is nearly eight years since this book was first published. I present it, unaltered, in the Cheap Edition; and such of my opinions as it expresses, are quite unaltered too.

My readers have opportunities of judging for themselves whether the influences and tendencies which I distrust in America, have any existence not in my imagination. They can examine for themselves whether there has been anything in the public career of that country during these past eight years, or whether there is anything in its present position, at home or abroad, which suggests that those influences and tendencies really do exist. As they find the fact, they will judge me. If they discern any evidence of wrong-going in any direction that I have indicated, they will acknowledge that I had reason in what I wrote. If they discern no such thing, they will consider me altogether mistaken.

Prejudiced, I never have been otherwise than in favour of the United States. No visitor can ever have set foot on those shores, with a stronger faith in the Republic than I had, when I landed in America.

I purposely abstain from extending these observations to any length. I have nothing to defend, or to explain away. The truth is the truth; and neither childish absurdities, nor unscrupulous contradictions, can make it otherwise. The earth would still move round the sun, though the whole Catholic Church said No.

I have many friends in America, and feel a grateful interest in the country. To represent me as viewing it with ill-nature, animosity, or partisanship, is merely to do a very foolish thing, which is always a very easy one: and which I have disregarded for eight years, and could disregard for eighty more.

LONDON, *June 22, 1850.*

---

75. "That other Public" in America

Published in Household Words, *3 February 1855. In this satirical piece Dickens speculates about "that other Public," which is always being exploited and cheated in its absurd gullibility but which never seems in evidence when the "real" public learns about such exploitation: "it is never forthcoming when [the public] is the subject of a joke at the theatre: which is always perceived to be a hit at some other Public richly deserving it, but not present." The " 'smart' Showman" to whom he alludes is the American P. T. Barnum, whose autobiography was published in 1855; Barnum exhibited, with enormous success, the dwarf, General Tom Thumb, in 1844 and handled a nationwide tour by Jenny Lind, the "Swedish nightingale," in 1850 to 1852. The "Old Granite State" is New Hampshire. See the last paragraph of extract 54 for the rest of the quotation at the end of this extract.*

There is one comfort in all this. We English are not the only victims of that other Public. It is to be heard of, elsewhere. It got across the Atlantic, in the train of the Pilgrim Fathers, and has frequently been achieving wonders in America. Ten or eleven years ago, one Chuzzlewit was heard to say, that he had found it on that side of the water, doing the strangest things. The assertion made all sorts of Publics angry, and there was quite a cordial combination of Publics to resent it and disprove it. But there *is* a little book of Memoirs to be heard of at the present time, which looks as if young Chuzzlewit had reason in him too. Does the 'smart' Showman, who makes such a Mermaid, and makes such a Washington's Nurse, and makes such a Dwarf, and makes such a Singing Angel upon earth, and makes such a fortune, and, above all, makes such a book – does *he* address the free and enlightened Public of the great United States: the Public of State Schools, Liberal Tickets, First-chop Intelligence, and Universal Education? No, no. That other Public is the sharks'-prey. It is that other Public, down somewhere or other, whose bright particular star and stripe are not yet ascertained, which is so transparently cheated and so hardily outfaced. For that other Public, the hatter of New York outbid Creation at the auction of the first Lind seat. For that other Public, the Lind speeches were made, the tears shed, the serenades given. It is that other Public, always on the boil and ferment about

"Welcome to Jenny Lind"

anything or nothing, whom the travelling companion shone down upon from the high Hotel-Balconies. It is that other Public who will read, and even buy, the smart book in which they have so proud a share, and who will fly into raptures about its being circulated from the old Ocean Cliffs of the Old Granite State to the Rocky Mountains. It is indubitably in reference to that other Public that we find the following passage in a book called *American Notes*. 'Another prominent feature is the love of "smart" dealing: which gilds over many a swindle and gross breach of trust; many a defalcation, public and private; and enables many a knave to hold his head up with the best, who well deserves a halter . . .'

76. Remembering American inns

From the first section of The Holly-Tree Inn, *the special Christmas number of* Household Words *for 1855.*

The Planters' House, St. Louis, where Dickens stayed

I put out to sea for the Inns of America, with their four hundred beds apiece, and their eight or nine hundred ladies and gentlemen at dinner every day. Again I stood in the bar-rooms thereof, taking my evening cobbler, julep, sling, or cocktail. Again I listened to my friend the General, – whom I had known for five minutes, in the course of which period he had made me intimate for life with two Majors, who again had made me intimate for life with three Colonels, who again had made me brother to twenty-two civilians, – again, I say, I listened to my friend the General, leisurely expounding the re-sources of the establishment, as to gentlemen's morning-room, Sir; ladies' morning-room, Sir; gentlemen's evening-room, Sir; ladies' eve-ning-room, Sir; ladies' and gentlemen's evening reuniting-room, Sir; music-room, Sir; reading-room, Sir; over four hundred sleeping-rooms, Sir; and the entire planned and finished within twelve calen-dar months from the first clearing off of the old encumbrances on the plot, at a cost of five hundred thousand dollars, Sir. Again I found, as to my individual way of thinking, that the greater, the more gor-geous, and the more dollarous the establishment was, the less desirable it was. Nevertheless, again I drank my cobbler, julep, sling, or cock-tail, in all good-will, to my friend the General, and my friends the Majors, Colonels, and civilians all; full well knowing that, whatever little motes my beamy eyes may have descried in theirs, they belong to a kind, generous, large-hearted, and great people.

V. Second impressions:
letters & farewell speech, 1867/68

77. Boston revisited

To his subeditor on All the Year Round, *W. H. Wills, 21 November 1867. Dickens was staying at the Parker House; in 1842 he had stayed at the Tremont.*

Boston, as a City, is enormously changed since I was here, and is far more mercantile. I do not yet notice any special difference in manners and customs between my old time and this time – except that there is more of New York in this fine City than there was of yore. The Hotel I stayed at in my first visit has now become contemptible. This is an establishment like one of our Termini Hotels, with the addition of an immense quantity of white marble floors. I live on the third storey – our three rooms together – and have hot and cold wa-

Dickens caricature by "Spy," Leslie Ward, 1870

ter laid on in a bath in my bedroom, and other comforts not known in my former experience. The cuisine is very good. The cost of living is enormous. Ten Pounds sterling a day for Dolby and me is by no means a large estimate. (It was our original calculation.) Happily, Dolby has seen reason to make up his mind that the less I am shown – for nothing – the better for the Readings! So I am fended off and kept – so far – unexpectedly quiet. In addition to which I must say that I have experienced – so far – not the slightest intrusiveness, and everywhere the greatest respect and consideration. There is the utmost curiosity about the Readings, and I should not wonder if they proved to be a great surprise, seeing that the general notion stops at a mere "Reading," book in hand.

---

78. Dining customs

To his elder daughter, Mary, 1 December 1867. For Mr. and Mrs. Fields see the introduction.

James Fields

Kate Fields

I have been going on very well. A horrible custom obtains in these parts of asking you to dinner somewhere at half-past two, and to supper somewhere else about eight. I have run this gauntlet more than once, and its effect is, that there is no day for any useful purpose, and that the length of the evening is multiplied by a hundred. Yesterday I dined with a club at half-past two, and came back here at half-past eight with a general impression that it was at least two o'clock in the morning. Two days before I dined with Longfellow at half-past two, and came back at eight, supposing it to be midnight. To-day we have a state dinner-party in our rooms at six, Mr. and Mrs. Fields, and Mr. and Mrs. Bigelow. (He is a friend of Forster's, and was American Minister in Paris.) There are no negro waiters here, all the servants are Irish – willing, but not able. The dinners and wines are very good. I keep our own rooms well ventilated by opening the windows, but no window is ever opened in the halls or passages, and they are so overheated by a great furnace, that they make me faint and sick. The air is like that of a pre-Adamite ironing-day in full blast. Your re-

spected parent is immensely popular in Boston society, and its cor-
diality and unaffected heartiness are charming. I wish I could carry
it with me.

---

79. New York revisited

*To Forster, 14 December 1867. The Fenians were an anti-British
secret association of Irishmen, formed simultaneously in Ireland by
James Stephens and in New York by John O'Mahony in 1857 with
the object of making Ireland a republic.*

The only portion that has even now come back to me, is the part of
Broadway in which the Carlton Hotel (long since destroyed) used to
stand. There is a very fine new park in the outskirts, and the number
of grand houses and splendid equipages is quite surprising. There are
hotels close here with 500 bedrooms and I don't know how many
boarders; but this hotel is quite as quiet as, and not much larger than,
Mivart's in Brook Street. My rooms are all en suite, and I come and
go by a private door and private staircase communicating with my
bed-room. The waiters are French, and one might be living in Paris.

.   .   .   .

The Fenian explosion at Clerkenwell was telegraphed here in a few
hours. I do not think there is any sympathy whatever with the Fenians on the part of the American people, though political adventurers
may make capital out of a show of it. But no doubt large sections of
the Irish population of this State are themselves Fenian; and the local
politics of the place are in a most depraved condition, if half of what
is said to me be true. I prefer not to talk of these things, but at odd
intervals I look round for myself. Great social improvements in respect of manners and forbearance have come to pass since I was here
before, but in public life I see as yet but little change.

80. Railroads, policemen, and newspapers

Top left
*Stereoscopic view
of Central Park*

Top right
*Stereoscopic view
from the East Riv-
er Bridge*

Bottom left
*Stereoscopic view
of a New York
scene*

Bottom right
*Stereoscopic view
of the elevated
railroad*

To Forster, 22 December 1867.

The railways are truly alarming. Much worse (because more worn I suppose) than when I was here before. We were beaten about yesterday, as if we had been aboard the Cuba. Two rivers have to be crossed, and each time the whole train is banged aboard a big steamer. The steamer rises and falls with the river, which the railroad don't do; and the train is either banged up hill or banged down hill. In coming off the steamer at one of these crossings yesterday, we were banged up such a height that the rope broke, and one carriage rushed back with a run down-hill into the boat again. I whisked out in a moment, and two or three others after me; but nobody else seemed to care about it. The treatment of the luggage is perfectly outrageous. Nearly every case I have is already broken. When we started from Boston yesterday, I beheld, to my unspeakable amazement, Scott, my dresser, leaning a flushed countenance against the wall of the car, and *weeping bitterly*. It was over my smashed writing-desk. Yet the arrangements for luggage are excellent, if the porters would not be beyond description reckless.

The halls are excellent. Imagine one holding two thousand people, seated with exact equality for every one of them, and every one seated separately. I have nowhere, at home or abroad, seen so fine a police as the police of New York; and their bearing in the streets is above all praise. On the other hand, the laws for regulation of public vehicles, clearing of streets, and removal of obstructions, are wildly outraged by the people for whose benefit they are intended. Yet there is undoubtedly improvement in every direction, and I am taking time to make up my mind on things in general. Let me add that I have been tempted out at three in the morning to visit one of the large police station-houses, and was so fascinated by the study of a horrible photograph-book of thieves' portraits that I couldn't shut it up. . . .

A good specimen of the sort of newspaper you and I know something of, came out in Boston here this morning. The editor had applied for our advertisements, saying that "it was at Mr. D's disposal for paragraphs." The advertisements were not sent; Dolby did not enrich its columns paragraphically; and among its news to-day is the item that "this chap calling himself Dolby got drunk down town last night, and was taken to the police station for fighting an Irishman!" I am sorry to say that I don't find anybody to be much shocked by this liveliness. . . . The Tribune is an excellent paper. Horace Greeley

William Cullen Bryant, editor of the Evening Post

is editor in chief, and a considerable shareholder too. All the people connected with it whom I have seen are of the best class. It is also a very fine property – but here the New York Herald beats it hollow, hollow, hollow! Another able and well edited paper is the New York Times. A most respectable journal too is Bryant's Evening Post, excellently written. There is generally a much more responsible and respectable tone than prevailed formerly, however small may be the literary merit, among papers pointed out to me as of large circulation. In much of the writing there is certainly improvement, but it might be more widely spread.

81. Contrasts

To his sister-in-law, Georgina Hogarth, from Boston, 4 January 1868. The Irish playwright Dion Boucicault (1822–1890) was a prolific writer of melodramas.

Dolby's business at night is a mere nothing, for these people are so accustomed to take care of themselves, that one of these immense audiences will fall into their places with an ease amazing to a frequenter of St. James's Hall. And the certainty with which they are all in, before I go on, is a very acceptable mark of respect. I must add, too, that although there is a conventional familiarity in the use of one's name in the newspapers as "Dickens," "Charlie," and what not, I do not in the least see that familiarity in the writers themselves. An inscrutable tone obtains in journalism, which a stranger cannot understand. If I say in common courtesy to one of them, when Dolby introduces, "I am much obliged to you for your interest in me," or so forth, he seems quite shocked, and has a bearing of perfect modesty and propriety. I am rather inclined to think that they suppose their printed tone to be the public's love of smartness, but it is immensely difficult to make out. All I can as yet make out is, that my perfect freedom from bondage, and at any moment to go on or leave off, or otherwise do as I like, is the only safe position to occupy.

Again; there are two apparently irreconcilable contrasts here. Down below in this hotel every night are the bar loungers, dram drinkers, drunkards, swaggerers, loafers, that one might find in a Boucicault play. Within half an hour is Cambridge, where a delightful domestic life – simple, self-respectful, cordial, and affectionate – is seen in an admirable aspect. All New England is primitive and puritanical. All about and around is a puddle of mixed human mud, with no such quality in it. Perhaps I may in time sift out some tolerably intelligible whole, but I certainly have not done so yet. It is a good sign, may be, that it all seems immensely more difficult to understand than it was when I was here before.

---

82. Changes

To Forster, 14 January 1868. The notoriously parochial "Marylebone vestry" was the local government for that area of London. "The Boot's story" was a reading derived from The Holly-Tree Inn, *the special Christmas number of* Household Words *for 1855.*

I see *great changes* for the better, socially. Politically, no. England governed by the Marylebone vestry and the penny papers, and England as she would be after years of such governing; is what I make of *that*. Socially, the change in manners is remarkable. There is much greater politeness and forbearance in all ways. . . . On the other hand there are still provincial oddities wonderfully quizzical; and the newspapers are constantly expressing the popular amazement at "Mr. Dickens's extraordinary composure." They seem to take it ill that I don't stagger on to the platform overpowered by the spectacle before me, and the national greatness. They are all so accustomed to do public things with a flourish of trumpets, that the notion of my coming in to read without somebody first flying up and delivering an "Oration" about me, and flying down again and leading me in, is so very unaccountable to them, that sometimes they have no idea until I open my lips that it can possibly be Charles Dickens. . . .

. . . The Irish element is acquiring such enormous influence in New York city, that when I think of it, and see the large Roman Catholic cathedral rising there, it seems unfair to stigmatise as "American" other monstrous things that one also sees. But the general corruption in respect of the local funds appears to be stupendous, and there is an alarming thing as to some of the courts of law which I am afraid is native-born. A case came under my notice the other day in which it was perfectly plain, from what was said to me by a person interested in resisting an injunction, that his first proceeding had been to "look up the Judge." . . . Last night here in Philadelphia (my first night), a very impressive and responsive audience were so astounded by my simply walking in and opening my book that I wondered what was the matter. They evidently thought that there ought to have been a flourish, and Dolby sent in to prepare for me. With them it is the simplicity of the operation that raises wonder. With the newspapers "Mr. Dickens's extraordinary composure" is not reasoned out as being necessary to the art of the thing, but is sensitively watched with a lurking doubt whether it may not imply disparagement of the audience. Both these things strike me as drolly expressive. . . .

I think it reasonable to expect that as I go westward, I shall find the old manners going on before me, and may tread upon their skirts mayhap. But so far, I have had no more intrusion or boredom than I have when I lead the same life in England. I write this in an immense hotel, but I am as much at peace in my own rooms, and am left as wholly undisturbed, as if I were at the Station Hotel in York. I have now read in New York city to 40,000 people, and am quite as well known in the streets there as I am in London. People will turn back, turn again and face me, and have a look at me, or will say to one another, "Look here! Dickens coming!" But no one ever stops me or addresses me. Sitting reading in the carriage outside the New York post-office while one of the staff was stamping the letters inside, I be-

Characters at Dickens' readings, published in Harper's Weekly, 25 April 1868.

1. The appreciative hearer, determined to show his enthusiasm.

2. The inquisitive hearer, who wishes to see the man that all the papers are talking about.

3. The spoony hearers, listening to "Dora and her Doady."

4. The Fellow Author, who wonders if he is recognised and read by Mr D.

5. The swindled hearer, who insists on relating his grievances.

6. The suggestive hearers – "Why, he looks like his own Dick Swiveller!"

came conscious that a few people who had been looking at the turn-out had discovered me within. On my peeping out good-humouredly, one of them (I should say a merchant's book-keeper) stepped up to the door, took off his hat, and said in a frank way: "Mr. Dickens, I should very much like to have the honour of shaking hands with you" – and, that done, presented two others. Nothing could be more quiet or less intrusive. In the railway cars, if I see anybody who clearly wants to speak to me, I usually anticipate the wish by speaking myself. If I am standing on the brake outside (to avoid the intolerable stove), people getting down will say with a smile: "As I am taking my departure, Mr. Dickens, and can't trouble you for more than a moment, I should like to take you by the hand, sir." And so we shake hands and go our ways. . . . Of course many of my impressions come through the readings. Thus I find the people lighter and more humorous than formerly; and there must be a great deal of innocent imagination among every class, or they never could pet with such extraordinary pleasure as they do, the Boots's story of the elopement of the two little children.

---

83. Baltimore postbellum

To Samuel Cartwright, 29 January 1868. Butler was a highly unpopular general of the Union army during the Civil War; he achieved great notoriety by ordering that any southern ladies who openly showed their hostility toward Union soldiers should be punished as common prostitutes.

This is one of the places where Butler carried it with so high a hand in the war, and where the ladies used to spit when they passed a Northern soldier. It still wears, I fancy, a look of sullen remembrance. (The ladies are remarkably handsome, with an Eastern look upon them, dress with a strong sense of colour, and make a brilliant audience.) The ghost of slavery haunts the houses; and the old, untidy, incapable, lounging, shambling black serves you as a free man. Free of course he ought to be; but the stupendous absurdity of making him a voter glares out of every roll of his eye, stretch of his mouth, and bump of his head. I have a strong impression that the race must fade out of the States very fast. It never can hold its own against a striving, restless, shifty people. In the penitentiary here, the other

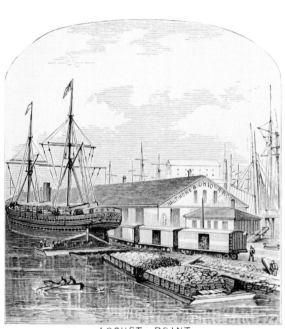

LOCUST POINT.

CALVERT STREET.

SPEAR'S WHARF.

EXCHANGE PLACE.

day, in a room full of all blacks (too dull to be taught any of the work in hand), was one young brooding fellow, very like a black rhinoceros. He sat glowering at life, as if it were just endurable at dinner time, until four of his fellows began to sing, most unmelodiously, a part song. He then set up a dismal howl, and pounded his face on a form. I took him to have been rendered quite desperate by having learnt anything.

---

84. The Ghost of Slavery

To Forster, 30 January 1868.

Dolby decided that the croakers were wrong about Washington, and went on; the rather as his raised prices, which he put finally at three dollars each, gave satisfaction. Fields is so confident about Boston, that my remaining list includes, in all, 14 more readings there. I don't know how many more we might not have had here (where I have had attentions otherwise that have been very grateful to me), if we had chosen. Tickets are now being resold at ten dollars each. At Baltimore I had a charming little theatre, and a very apprehensive impulsive audience. It is remarkable to see how the Ghost of Slavery haunts the town; and how the shambling, untidy, evasive, and postponing Irrepressible proceeds about his free work, going round and round it, instead of at it. The melancholy absurdity of giving these people votes, at any rate at present, would glare at one out of every roll of their eyes, chuckle in their mouths, and bump in their heads, if one did not see (as one cannot help seeing in the country) that their enfranchisement is a mere party trick to get votes. Being at the Penitentiary the other day (this, while we mention votes), and looking over the books, I noticed that almost every man had been "pardoned" a day or two before his time was up. Why? Because, if he had served his time out, he would have been *ipso facto* disfranchised. So, this form of pardon is gone through to save his vote; and as every officer of the prison holds his place only in right of his party, of course his hopeful clients vote for the party that has let them out! When I read in Mr. Beecher's church at Brooklyn, we found the trustees had suppressed the fact that a certain upper gallery holding 150 was "the Coloured Gallery." On the first night not a soul could be induced to enter it; and it was not until it became known next day

"A MAN AND A BROTHER."

Uncle Sam.—" WAL, CHARLEY, I GUESS YOU'RE WELCOME; LET ME INTRODUCE TO YOU OUR NEW BROTHER FROM DOWN SOUTH—'THE MOST REMARKABLE MAN IN THE COUNTRY.'"

Cartoon published in the London illustrated comic paper Banter, *26 December 1867*

that I was certainly not going to read there more than four times, that we managed to fill it. One night at New York, on our second or third row, there were two well-dressed women with a tinge of colour – I should say, not even quadroons. But the holder of one ticket who found his seat to be next them, demanded of Dolby "What he meant by fixing him next to those two Gord darned cusses of niggers?" and insisted on being supplied with another good place. Dolby firmly replied that he was perfectly certain Mr. Dickens would not recognise such an objection on any account, but he could have his money back if he chose. Which, after some squabbling, he had. In a comic scene in the New York circus one night, when I was looking on, four white people sat down upon a form in a barber's shop to be shaved. A coloured man came as the fifth customer, and the four immediately ran away. This was much laughed at and applauded. In the Baltimore Penitentiary, the white prisoners dine on one side of the room, the coloured prisoners on the other; and no one has the slightest idea of mixing them. But it is indubitably the fact that exhalations not the most agreeable arise from a number of coloured people got together, and I was obliged to beat a quick retreat from their dormitory.

85. President Johnson

To Forster, 7 February 1868. Andrew Johnson was Lincoln's vice-president and became president after Lincoln's assassination. Webster was Daniel Webster (1782–1852), an American statesman whom Dickens had met both in London and America. Carlyle described him thus: "a grim, tall, broad-bottomed, yellow-skinned man, with brows like precipitous cliffs and huge, black, dull, wearied yet unweariable-looking eyes under them; amorphous projecting nose, and the angriest shut mouth I have anywhere seen." Sir Edward Thornton was British ambassador to the United States.

President Andrew Johnson

This scrambling scribblement is resumed this morning, because I have just seen the President who had sent to me very courteously asking me to make my own appointment. He is a man with a remarkable face, indicating courage, watchfulness, and certainly strength of purpose. It is a face of the Webster type, but without the "bounce" of Webster's face. I would have picked him out anywhere as a character of mark. Figure, rather stoutish for an American; a trifle under the middle size; hands clasped in front of him; manner, suppressed, guarded, anxious. Each of us looked at the other very hard. . . . It was in his own cabinet that I saw him. As I came away, Thornton drove up in a sleigh – turned out for a state occasion – to deliver his credentials. There was to be a cabinet council at 12. The room was very like a London club's ante-drawing room. On the walls, two engravings only: one, of his own portrait; one, of Lincoln's. . . . In the outer room was sitting a certain sunburnt General Blair, with many evidences of the war upon him. He got up to shake hands with me, and then I found that he had been out on the Prairie with me five-and-twenty years ago. . . . The papers having referred to my birthday's falling to-day, my room is filled with most exquisite flowers. They came pouring in from all sorts of people at breakfast time. The audiences here are really very fine. So ready to laugh or cry, and doing both so freely, that you would suppose them to be Manchester shillings rather than Washington half-sovereigns. Alas! alas! my cold worse than ever.

---

86. Syracuse

To Georgina Hogarth, 8 March 1868.

This is a very grim place in a heavy thaw, and a most depressing one. The hotel also is surprisingly bad, quite a triumph in that way. We stood out for an hour in the melting snow, and came in again, having to change completely. Then we sat down by the stove (no fireplace), and there we are now. We were so afraid to go to bed last night, the rooms were so close and sour, that we played whist, double dummy, till we couldn't bear each other any longer. We had an old buffalo for supper, and an old pig for breakfast, and we are going to have I don't know what for dinner at six. In the public rooms downstairs, a number of men (speechless) are sitting in rocking-chairs, with their feet against the window-frames, staring out at window and spitting dolefully at intervals. Scott is in tears, and George the gasman is suborning people to go and clean the hall, which is a marvel of dirt.

Pages 240–241
Syracuse

87. Buffalo

To Forster, 13 March 1868.

This Buffalo has become a large and important town, with numbers of German and Irish in it. But it is very curious to notice, as we touch the frontier, that the American female beauty dies out; and a woman's face clumsily compounded of German, Irish, Western America, and Canadian, not yet fused together, and not yet moulded, obtains instead. Our show of Beauty at night is, generally, remarkable; but we had not a dozen pretty women in the whole throng last night, and the faces were all blunt. I have just been walking about, and observing the same thing in the streets. . . . The winter has been so severe, that the hotel on the English side at Niagara (which has the best view of the Falls, and is for that reason very preferable) is not yet open. So we go, perforce, to the American; which telegraphs back to our tele-

The old Elk Street Market in Buffalo, 1855

gram: "all Mr. Dickens's requirements perfectly understood." I have not yet been in more than two *very bad* inns. I have been in some, where a good deal of what is popularly called "slopping round" has prevailed; but have been able to get on very well. "Slopping round," so used, means untidyness and disorder. It is a comically expressive phrase, and has many meanings. Fields was asking the price of a quarter-cask of sherry the other day. "Wa'al Mussr Fields," the merchant replies, "that varies according to quality, as is but nay'tral. If yer wa'ant a sherry just to slop round with it, I can fix you some at a very low figger."

---

88. Last words in America

Speech at a banquet in his honour given by the New York Press Association at Delmonico's. Sir Anthony Absolute is a leading character in Sheridan's The Rivals.

Gentlemen, so much of my voice has lately been heard in the land, and I have for upwards of four hard winter months so contended against what I have been sometimes quite admiringly assured was 'a true American catarrh' [*laughter*] – a possession which I have throughout highly appreciated, though I might have preferred to be naturalized by any other outward and visible means. [*Shouts of laughter.*] I say, gentlemen, so much of my voice has lately been heard, that I might have been contented with troubling you no further from my present standing-point, were it not a duty with which I henceforth charge myself, not only here but on every suitable occasion, whatsoever and wheresoever, to express my high and grateful sense of my second reception in America, and to bear my honest testimony to the national generosity and magnanimity. [*Great applause.*] Also, to declare how astounded I have been by the amazing changes that I have seen around me on every side – changes moral, changes physical, changes in the amount of land subdued and peopled, changes in the rise of vast new cities, changes in the growth of older cities almost out of recognition, changes in the graces and amenities of life, changes in the Press, without whose advancement no advancement can be made anywhere. [*Applause.*] Nor am I, believe me, so arrogant as to suppose that in five-and-twenty years there have been no changes in me, and that I have nothing to learn, and that I had nothing to learn and no extreme impressions to correct from when I was here first. [*A voice – 'Noble,' and applause.*]

And, gentlemen, this brings me to a point on which I have, ever since I landed here last November, observed a strict silence, though sometimes tempted to break it, but in reference to which I will, with your permission, beg leave to take you now into my confidence. [*Laughter and applause – cries of 'Silence'.*] Even the Press, being human [*laughter*], may be sometimes mistaken or misinformed, and I rather think that I have myself, on one or two occasions, in some rare instances, known its information to be not perfectly accurate with reference to myself. [*Laughter and applause.*] Indeed, I have now and again been more surprised by printed news that I have read of myself, than by any printed news that I have ever read in my present state of existence. [*Laughter.*] Thus, the vigour and perseverance with which I have for some months past been collecting materials and hammering away at a new book on America have much astonished me [*renewed laughter*]; seeing that all that time it has been perfectly well known to my publishers on both sides of the Atlantic, that I positively declared that no consideration on earth should induce me to write one. But what I have intended, what I have resolved upon (and this is the confidence I seek to place in you) is, on my return to England, in my own person to bear, for the behoof of my countrymen, such testimony to the gigantic changes in this country as I have hinted at tonight. [*Immense applause.*] Also, to record that wherever I have been, in the smallest places equally with the largest, I have been received with unsurpassable politeness, delicacy, sweet temper, hospitality, consideration, and with unsurpassable respect for the privacy daily enforced upon me by the nature of my avocation here, and the state of my health. [*Applause.*] This testimony, so long as I live, and so long as my descendants have any legal right in my books, I shall cause to be republished, as an appendix to every copy of those two books of mine in which I have referred to America. [*Tremendous applause.*] And this I will do and cause to be done, not in mere love and thankfulness, but because I regard it as an act of plain justice and honour ['*Bravo!*' *and cheers.*]

Gentlemen, the transition from my own feelings towards and interest in America to those of the mass of my countrymen seems to be a natural one; but, whether or no, I make it with an express object. I was asked in this very city, about last Christmas time, whether an American was not at some disadvantage in England as a foreigner. The notion of an American being regarded in England as a foreigner at all, of his ever being thought of or spoken of in that character, was so uncommonly incongruous and absurd to me, that my gravity was

The press dinner for Dickens at Delmonico's, 1868. Sketched by Thomas Nast

for the moment quite overpowered. [*Laughter*.] As soon as it was restored, I said that for years and years past I hoped I had had as many American friends and had received as many American visitors as almost any Englishman living, and that my unvarying experience, fortified by theirs, was that it was enough in England to be an American to be received with the readiest respect and recognition anywhere. [*Applause*.] Hereupon, out of half a dozen people, suddenly spoke out two, one an American gentleman, with a cultivated taste for art, who, finding himself on a certain Sunday outside the walls of a certain historical English castle, famous for its pictures, was refused admission there, according to the strict rules of the establishment on that day, but who, on merely representing that he was an American gentleman on his travels, had, not to say the picture gallery, but the whole castle, placed at his immediate disposal. [*Laughter*.] The other was a lady who, being in London, and having a great desire to see the famous reading-room of the British Museum, was assured by the English family with whom she stayed that it was unfortunately impossible, because the place was closed for a week, and she had only three days there. Upon that lady's going to the Museum, as she assured me, alone to the gate, self-introduced as an American lady, the gate flew open, as it were magically. [*Laughter and applause.*] I am unwillingly bound to add that she certainly was young and exceedingly pretty. [*Laughter.*] Still, the porter of that institution is of an obese habit [*laughter*], and, according to the best of my observation of him, not very impressible. [*Great laughter and cheering.*]

Now, gentlemen, I refer to these trifles as a collateral assurance to you that the Englishman who shall humbly strive, as I hope to do, to be in England as faithful to America as to England herself, has no previous conceptions to contend against. [*'Good!' 'Good!' and cheers.*] Points of difference there have been, points of difference there are, points of difference there probably always will be between the two great peoples. But broadcast in England is sown the sentiment that those two peoples are essentially one [*great applause*], and that it rests with them jointly to uphold the great Anglo-Saxon race, to which our President has referred, and all its great achievements before the world. [*'Bravo!' and applause.*] And if I know anything of my countrymen – and they give me credit for knowing something – if I know anything of my countrymen, gentlemen, the English heart is stirred by the fluttering of those Stars and Stripes, as it is stirred by no other flag that flies except its own. [*Tremendous applause, and three cheers.*] If I know my countrymen, in any and every relation towards America, they begin, not as Sir Anthony Absolute recommended that lovers should begin, with 'a little aversion', but with a great liking and profound respect [*applause*]; and whatever the little sensitiveness of the moment, or the little official passion, or the little official policy now, or then, or here, or there, may be, take my word for it, that the first enduring, great popular consideration in England is a generous construction of justice. [*'Bravo!' and cheers.*]

Finally, gentlemen, and I say this subject to your correction, I do believe that from the great majority of honest minds on both sides, there cannot be absent the conviction that it would be better for this globe to be riven by an earthquake, fired by a comet, overrun by an iceberg, and abandoned to the Arctic fox and bear, than that it should present the spectacle of these two great nations each of which has, in its own way and hour, striven so hard and so successfully for freedom, ever again being arrayed the one against the other. [*Tumultuous applause, the company rising and cheering.*]

Dickens caricature by "Spy," Leslie Ward, 1870

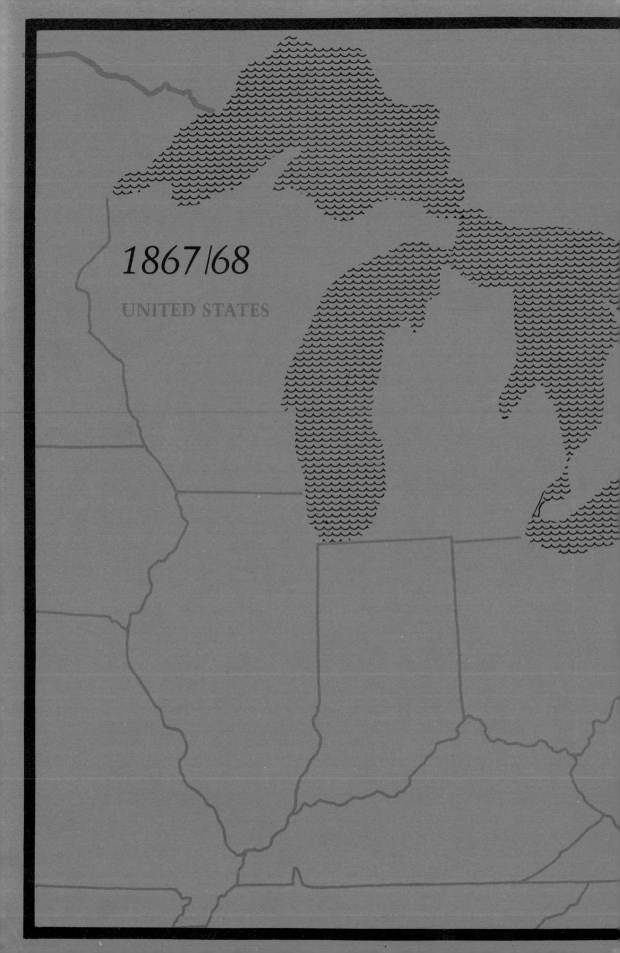

1867/68

UNITED STATES